# BUT THAT'S ANOTHER STORY...

Ann,

I am so happy that you want me to autograph this book —

Best wishes to you & Bob

Maralla

# BUT THAT'S ANOTHER STORY...

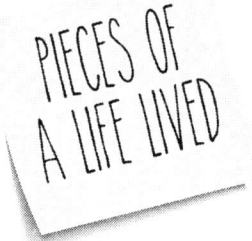

*a memoir by*
MARCELLA ANN STAPOR

*But That's Another Story*
First Edition

Copyright © 2016 by Marcella Ann Stapor
All international rights reserved.

No part of this publication may be reproduced, stored in a retrieval system, or transmitted in any form by any means, electronic, mechanical, photocopying, recording or otherwise, without the prior written permission of the author.

Published in the United States of America by Legacy Projects

ISBN–13: 978-1539753322
ISBN–10: 1539753328

Cover and interior design by Bruce Kluger

Unless otherwise noted, all photographs courtesy of Marcella Ann Stapor

*For Brendan, Charlie, William, Jack and Emma Grace*

## CONTENTS

| | |
|---|---|
| **Foreword** | iii |
| **A Note to Readers** | v |
| **Seventy-Five!** | 1 |
| Celebrate! • What's Next? • My Greatest Challenge | |
| *TRANSITIONS: Traveling Is My Religion* | 13 |
| **Giving Back** | 17 |
| The Best of Intentions • On a Deeper Level • An Afghan Girl • "Gorgeous" | |
| *TRANSITIONS: A Great Train Ride* | 30 |
| **Condo Board Woes** | 35 |
| Reconsidering the Board | |
| *TRANSITIONS: The Arabian Gulf* | 40 |
| **Career** | 45 |
| Breaking Barriers?! • Gender Gap • Violation • My Almost Second Career • Expanding My Resume | |
| *TRANSITIONS: Rosh Hashanah 5771* | 58 |
| **Relationships** | 61 |
| Marriage...? | |
| *TRANSITIONS: Where Were You on 9/11?* | 71 |

## Law School
What a Challenge! ....... 75

*TRANSITIONS: Trouble in Taormina* ....... 81

## Family
My Immigrant Grandparents • Oil and Water • Leena and Neena • My Father…A Mixed Legacy • Childhood World • Loretta • Sister Ligouria • Becoming Aunt Alice • Gizmo and Harley • My Ballet Debut • I Like to Work! • The Search Is Over • Gwen • An Ethical Dilemma ....... 87

*TRANSITIONS: Scammed?* ....... 138

## Health
Mission Accomplished—Finally! • Heat! • Like Father, Unlike Daughter ....... 141

*TRANSITIONS: Stitches!* ....... 152

## Reflections
Morning Routine • A Love Affair with Autumn • My To Do List ....... 157

*TRANSITIONS: On Spirituality* ....... 165

## Gratitude
Love and Fear and Karma • Wanted: A Crystal Ball! • I Am Grateful For… ....... 169

*TRANSITIONS: Moved to Tears* ....... 176

## Epilogue ....... 179

## Acknowledgments ....... 181

## FOREWORD

Before you begin reading, we would like you to know that Marcella is our treasured aunt and has been a big influence on our lives since childhood.

One story that comes to mind is how she adopts old, sick cats and takes care of them when no one else will.

We also remember well the trips she took us on to places like Iceland, Ireland and Alaska, as well as introducing us to new cuisines and cultural events.

If we were to write a book about her, we might call it *Our Auntie Mame* and we know that you will soon find our firsthand what we're talking about. You will learn through our aunt's living example that a woman's success and happiness is not dependent on anyone and that you can achieve your goals no matter what obstacles come your way.

Our aunt has overcome tremendous gender bias and remained steadfast in living life on her own terms.

We are so excited that you now have the chance to get to know her.

—Carol Sue, Alice Ann and JP

## NOTE TO READER

The genesis of this book began in a writing class I took over several years at The Ethical Culture Society. My teacher, who I thank in the Acknowledgments, prompted us to write about a variety of subjects, from cats to health to family and career, along with a host of themes in between, including running a condo board, volunteering at a VA hospital and our personal connections to 9/11.

Many of these topics appear in singular essays, while others keep popping up again and again, like my travels and my relationships, in no particular order, but all reflecting the significance each of them has played in my life.

I've cobbled these pieces together in a way that I think demonstrates how I have actually lived. Most of the names are real, but a few have been changed.

I hope you enjoy it.

*Marcella Ann Hyper*

New York City
Fall 2016

*Seventy-Five!*

# Celebrate!

BACK IN THE 1980's, I used to invite my teenage nephew living in Katonah, Westchester, and two of his best high school friends to spend weekends in the city with me. I would take JP and the boys to their preferred movie and then to an ethnic restaurant of my choice in an effort to widen their experience and expand their palette. They loved it all.

One weekend night, something unusual happened. After dinner, we returned to the apartment and I retired to my bedroom and promptly fell asleep. All too soon, the phone woke me up and I heard the voice of my building's concierge.

"Do you have three boys here as guests?"

"Yes!"

"They're in the lobby. Can you come get them, please, and bring them back to your apartment?"

As I was not dressed I asked him to kindly put them in the elevator so I could greet them on my floor. When they got to me on the third floor, we walked quietly to my apartment. Obviously, something was going on. I could see it on their faces.

"Let's sit on the floor," I said, as soon as we got inside, "and you three tell me what happened."

According to the boys, after I went to bed they decided to go up on the roof of the building. It sounded okay so far. Then they shared that they'd also taken rolls of toilet paper up there with them, where they'd wadded up the paper into balls and threw them down 14 floors onto the passing cars.

One ball hit the balcony of the penthouse below the roof. A man suddenly appeared on the roof, pointing a gun at all three boys, and started yelling about calling the police. He ordered the boys to lie face down on the roof's tarmac, which they did. Then he called the super who came up immediately. Luckily for me, the super recognized the boys as my guests and told them to come with him to the lobby.

The man from the penthouse followed them. That's when my phone rang. Once I had the boys safely in my apartment, I wasn't really mad at them—*come on, guys, toilet paper? Really?* But I was enraged about the man and his gun. After the boys left the next day, I wrote a note to the penthouse owner informing him that if he called the police over the boys' prank I would counter with an allegation against him of assault with a deadly weapon. I never heard back from him or any police.

Many years later, as our memories can often fast-forward, I was about to celebrate my 75th birthday. It was October 11, 2012. A month earlier, my nephew, now living in Los Angeles, announced that he would be flying in to New York for the weekend to celebrate my birthday. I tried to talk him out of making the trip but he insisted. As I had already made plans for a Circle Line cruise up the Hudson River to Bear Mountain for that Saturday, I told my nephew that I would purchase a ticket for him, too.

Meanwhile, my friend Gwen, who lives in Bath, England, and who has been a good friend for almost 50 years, had called to say she was also coming. Since she was 84 years old, I tried to talk her out of it, feeling that it would be too much for her. But she insisted. She was arriving on October 9th and staying till the 19th, which was fine.

The celebrating didn't wait. It began on October 6th when my nieces came to the city to take me out for an early birthday dinner. When Gwen arrived a few days later, we did touristy things each day, like the Circle Line tour of Manhattan, visiting the 9/11 memorial and walking around the city as much as we could! On my actual birthday, a neighbor threw a dinner party with other friends I have made in my apartment building, which ended with a lovely birthday cake and candle blowing.

Did the celebration end on that evening? No!

On Saturday, Gwen and JP joined me at the boat for our trip upstate. Once we got seated on board, JP put his jacket over two other seats but I thought nothing of it. He said he wanted to explore the ship and just before our departure he returned to our seats. I was busy chatting with Gwen when suddenly I saw two men walking toward me. I recognized them as JP's best friends from high school, the same boys who got caught throwing toilet paper off the roof before being threatened by an overzealous neighbor.

We had not seen each other in about 20 years though I kept track of where they lived and what they were doing. JP captured the event on his camera and forwarded the video to his sisters—my beautiful nieces—as they were in on the whole surprise and had been waiting for the video to see my shocked expression. I didn't disappoint them!

The dinners and brunches that followed were filled with multiple stories, but the one that stood out was a repeat of that "man with the gun" incident. All three boys—now men—kept saying how grateful they were for how I reacted and that joining me for my 75th birthday was just one way to acknowledge that. One had flown in from D.C. and the other lives in the city. I was elated to have them with me.

Our celebrations lasted until Gwen left for the U.K. This was one of the longest birthday parties I'd ever had, and while it was great fun it also kept me thinking for 15 straight days about reaching the age of 75.

Now that that milestone is over and all is back to quiet times, I can think of other things and just move on!

## What's Next?

When I stop practicing law and retire, which I hope can be soon, I wonder what I might do with all that extra time on my hands. I want to stay busy so I have been pondering the possibilities. Should I do pro bono legal work? Should I volunteer with a non-profit organization? Maybe I should look for a part-time job that pays.

Every time I watch *Law and Order* on TV, I think about how much I would love to be a juror in one of those courtrooms.

Recently one day, as I stepped outside my condominium to run an errand, I was stopped in my tracks by the presence of two huge buses parked right in front of the building. I approached the drivers standing nearby, talking. I wanted to know who gave them permission to park these monstrous vehicles in front of a residential building.

The drivers pointed out that I couldn't prevent them from parking on a public street and that they would not be there long. I was curious, so I continued asking questions about who they were waiting for and where were they going.

"We're driving to Bedford," one driver said.

"Why Bedford?"

This town is known as a quiet bedroom community of professionals who commute into the city to work. I couldn't imagine who was going to get on these buses and why they would be going there, of all places.

"We're taking "extras" there for a movie shoot," one of the men said.

"Oh my goodness," I replied. "Extras?"

The men nodded.

"For a movie? Or TV?"

The men smiled and nodded. I had always wondered how extras got work and I guess my curiosity must have showed. One of the drivers suggested I talk to a fellow who was standing by my building.

"He's one of them," he said, pointing to the young man.

I immediately walked away from the drivers and introduced myself to one of the extras who was waiting on my street corner for a bus to take him to the site in Bedford.

"How did you get to be an extra?"

He proceeded to tell me about books I could buy that listed casting agents and the website *nycasting.com*, where I could sign up to get this work and then check their daily posting looking for professional acting talent and background extras.

"Make sure to always have a book or a puzzle," he said, "because there is a lot of waiting around."

"Thank you," I said, as I watched him plug in his earphones and go back to his reading material.

Within days, I bought the book, joined the site, created a resume with all my jobs, studies and "special skills" and even posted a photo a niece had taken of me over Christmas. I read the listings daily to see what might be suitable for a woman my age. I applied for a few but it took a while before I finally got a response.

When I read the email I was so excited one would think I had just won the lottery. Even though extras do not speak on camera I was already clearing space in the living room for my Oscar. My sister had been an extra and since she had a degree in nursing her first gig was playing a nurse in a hospital. Over the course of a couple of years she appeared in seven movies. Now it was my turn to walk down a street for an independent film being made in New York City.

My first day of shooting I had to report at seven a.m. to an exotic bird and plant shop on West 87th Street just down the street from where I lived—a real plus. When I arrived, there were already quite a few men and women gathered in the front of the shop. I asked one of them where to go and I was greeted warmly and taken to a food area inside where someone placed a chair for me. I already knew that there is always tons of food available all day on film shoots so I made myself comfortable, grabbed a bite, took out a book and began passing the time reading. An assistant director told us that our outdoor shot would likely take place in the morning but since it had started to snow outside some changes might be made in the order of shooting the scheduled scenes.

I saw women everywhere with laptops apparently working on the film but it was impossible to figure out exactly what it was they were doing. There appeared to be about 30 people working in the crew. The director, I was told, was somewhat famous in India and this was his first visit to New York City. Turns out, he came from Chennai and I told him I had been there on one of my two visits to India so that made for a nice little conversation.

The crew enjoyed engaging the extras in conversation. From the front of the store, I kept hearing instructions like "Quiet on the set" and "Camera rolling" and "Action," which meant you could not talk at all until you heard the word "Cut!"

Depending on where the shot was being filmed, these orders were repeated by different assistant directors. Then another assistant director (AD) would say the same thing in a different part of the store until finally someone where I was sitting would repeat the instructions. This went on for quite a few hours and no one told us extras when our scene would be shot. About four hours after I arrived, the AD who handled us came over and said they would be shooting the outside scene around noon. But lunch came and went, and after the crew ate we were invited to eat, which I guess is protocol on a film set. The Mexican food with all the fixings turned out to be delicious.

One of the most interesting parts of the day was meeting the man who ran the store. He loved exotic birds and reptiles and while one could buy the critters he really adopted them to save them. He was not making a profit but he didn't seem to care. Throughout the day, these creatures, all in cages, made incredibly loud sounds. but since the script for the movie called for the actors to be in an exotic bird store the sounds became part of the audio even while they were filming. I don't know the names of these birds except for the cockatiels, which were being sold for $175 each.

Finally, we were called around three p.m. to go outside. By this point, the snow had made its mark and I did not have any boots. We trudged out anyway and were given instructions for the scene. I was asked to walk to the middle of Amsterdam Avenue between 86th and 87th Street, turn around and when I heard the word "Action" I should start making my way through the snow and head toward the camera. Of course I never looked at the camera, which was the correct thing to do. Two paid male actors were in back of me having a conversation, which was being recorded. My job was to appear as someone passing by. The shot took all of 15 seconds but there was a problem getting the audio so we did "my big scene" three times.

After the shoot was over, we were told to stay because there may be another scene for us. We went back in the store and resumed our reading. A couple hours later, we heard "It's a wrap," which meant we could go. On the way out, we were told that we could come back for other extra work, as they would be shooting for another few weeks.

I pondered coming back and decided I would not, but the next morning I went online and replied to other casting calls to be a customer in a bookstore, a mourner at a funeral home and a juror in a courtroom. While I knew there was no pay for these roles in relatively low-budget independent films, I thought that putting them on my resume might eventually lead me to a paid job and a chance for union membership. Maybe I could even make a real income from this type of work. If I get this acting thing together, this might be what I will do as a retiree. Meanwhile, I will certainly get a lot of reading done, and one of these days I may even get a chance to do a stint in the courtroom on *Law and Order*.

Then again, maybe that's not the best use of my time.

## My Greatest Challenge

Yann Arthus-Bertrand is a French ecologist and journalist who is concerned about our environment. His 2009 documentary *Home* shows how mankind has caused the earth's erosion and claims that we have only ten years to undo the damage. Otherwise, the earth will self-destruct.

As the film begins, we see an aerial view of Iceland, showing a piece of the earth's terrain that has been untouched since its beginning. Except for one scene, all of the shots in the film are taken from a plane and are accompanied by Glenn Close's voiceover, explaining what we are witnessing.

Arthus-Bertrand filmed scenes in 60 countries to tell the story. Some of the topics covered are oxygen, water, plant life, trees, fish and animals and how these elements originally created—and continue to maintain—the balance that makes our world exist as it does. He also discusses how we are destroying that balance.

For instance, I found it very interesting to learn that among all the new skyscrapers going up in Dubai, which is a sun-rich environment, not one of them is powered by solar panels.

This film gave me a sense of doom, even though there was an attempt to show that there are some efforts, like windmills in Denmark that are being made to slow down the earth's erosion.

*Home* is intended to create a better understanding of our earth and this starts at the grassroots level. You can see the entire film online for free. I guarantee you will be profoundly moved!

I spent many years studying religions of all kinds, looking for a purpose for my life. Although I did not find an answer, I always felt that there was one out there and that I just hadn't stumbled across it—yet.

I've concluded that whatever the answer is I will just try to live a moral life. But after seeing this film I thought that if we are living on an earth that is being destroyed, what's the point of looking for a purpose?

My greatest life challenge has been to simply live without knowing anything conclusive about this idea of a purpose. At least now I will consciously do as little as possible to contribute to the earth's destruction and I will consider that a purpose, perhaps even a noble one.

## *Traveling Is My Religion*

*It's one world, not a lot of little worlds.*

That's what I thought when I first noticed the spirituality of traveling while flying in an airplane and marveling at the vast site below us. I saw the connectedness of it all. There simply cannot be *one* right religion.

While attending Catholic grammar school I queried two things: the virgin birth and the Catholic church's claim that it was the only religion that could "save" people from a life in hell, if there even is such a place. (I'm glad to report that the latter is no longer espoused.)

Even with these two questions, I was a faithful practicing Catholic. One friend of mine reminds me from time to time about a Saturday matinee performance of the ballet we attended together at the City Center theater back in the 1960's. She vividly remembers that I left early to attend a 5:30 p.m. Mass. Then, one Sunday about a year later (I was about 30), I was sitting in a pew awaiting Mass but I did not see an altar. I saw a stage and when the priest appeared I saw him wearing a costume, not a vestment. It was a very eerie feeling and I left the church that day before the Mass started.

I do not know if my travels all over Europe before this particular Sunday had anything to do with my altered perception inside the church but I suspect it did. Even though I am not fluent in a language other than English, traveling had enabled me to view other peoples' worlds—even superficially. I found that people everywhere, with the exception of Buddhist monks and similar communities, were doing the same things: marrying, having children, working.

Then one day I learned about The Century Club, based in Los Angeles. I downloaded their application and noted that one could join only after having been to 100 jurisdictions. I was excited and checked off all the places I had traveled to up until that time—75! I was disappointed, but I knew I had more destinations in mind, so maybe one day I would reach 100 places and have the chance to join a club with others who might be having the same experience of adventure and spiritual oneness.

I've continued to enjoy many trips but I no longer need or want to join The Century Club. While that was my goal for many years, it no longer seems so important. It's just a club and I am not really a joiner. In fact, I am a loner, but this does not change my view of the world. My travels have led me to conclude that everyone is on a path to live life with meaning. Even criminals, terrorists and scam artists are doing the same thing—except the particular path they have chosen is not one I condone.

Although in the future I may opt for less expensive trips or go on volunteer vacations, I probably won't stop traveling because it is my religion. Each time I travel and discover another new little world, it reconnects me with that feeling of oneness.

But that's another story...

*Giving Back*

## The Best of Intentions

HURRICANE SANDY passed by my apartment building in New York City and luckily, it left no scars. But since the devastation was rampant throughout Long Island, the Rockaways and especially Staten Island, I felt compelled to do something. When I got an email from an organization offering possibilities to volunteer, one of the places helping hurricane victims was the Alice Austen Museum on Staten Island. I had never heard of her or the museum, but I decided that visiting there would be an interesting experience where I could do some good and visit a part of my city I have never seen.

On Thanksgiving Sunday, I took the train to the ferry—well, not quite—as the #1 train no longer ends there—another casualty of Sandy. One has to get off at Rector Street and walk a long way to the terminal. After a nice ride across the river enjoying the incredible rearview skyline of Lower Manhattan, I got off the ferry and boarded a bus, just as the volunteer website directed. I asked the driver to let me off at Hylan Boulevard. Along the way, I saw areas with a lot of storm debris, including garage doors that had come unhinged, damaged cars and piles of ruined furniture. I saw people outside doing whatever they could. At one point, we passed quite a few trucks that were giving away food, water and clothing.

About 25 minutes later, we arrived at Hylan and as I disembarked I looked around for the addresses of the various buildings and quickly noted that the numbers were in the 2000 range instead of number 2 Hylan Boulevard, the address of the museum where I had been instructed to go. In previous email exchanges I had asked for directions and was told to look on the main website where all my questions would be answered. I searched the site and wrote down the address and directions, along with two telephone numbers.

But none of that seemed helpful at the time and I became frustrated, wondering what to do. After all, I was in a strange part of the world, having never been beyond the ferry terminal on Staten Island. After some bewildering minutes, I noticed two policewomen in a McDonald's parking lot and I flagged them down. They knew about the Alice Austen Museum but pointed out that I was at the wrong end of Hylan Boulevard and would need to take a different bus that stopped nearby.

I thanked them and called the museum while waiting at the bus stop, intending to ask if they still needed me or if enough volunteers had already shown up for the day. If that were the case, I thought I would just head home. All I got was a message. No one picked up the second line so I figured I would still try to get to the museum.

What appeared to be the right bus came whizzing by and didn't stop. I was stunned, but then I thought it must have kept going because I didn't stand up and motion for the driver to stop. I realized this was necessary since this was a stop for several different buses.

I sat back down to wait again, grateful that I had doubled up on clothing because I did not know if the volunteer work was inside or outside. The extra clothing really helped keep me comfortable in the cold weather.

Finally, another bus came along and I flagged the driver down. About ten minutes later we were in the 1000 block of Hylan and ten minutes more had us in the 500's. Then all of a sudden the bus turned off Hylan when it was in the 400's, still nowhere near number two!

I had noted when I boarded this bus that its last stop on this route was the ferry terminal. Need I say more?

Upon returning to my apartment, I emailed the contact person at the Museum to tell her what happened.

"Oh, yes," she responded. "There are two occasions where the bus meets Hylan Boulevard and the one you found yourself on was the wrong end of this road."

*Why didn't she think to tell me that in the first place?*

You might also be wondering what I thought of Staten Island. Well, that's definitely a story for another day.

## On a Deeper Level

Many years ago, I volunteered one night a week at the Veterans Hospital in midtown, where I talked with the patients and handed out juice.

One day, a nurse informed me that a new patient had arrived, and if I could I should give him more attention than the other patients. She explained that he was a doctor who worked in that very hospital. She also said he had taken a vacation recently and spent it volunteering in a hospital in Nigeria until the car he was in got hit by a truck, which resulted in his having broken every bone in his body. As soon as the doctors in Nigeria thought he could be moved, he was flown back to the U.S. and brought to this Veterans Hospital.

"Please give him your attention," said the nurse, as she gave me his room number.

I went immediately to see him and found a man all wrapped up in bandages and blankets and casts. He could hardly talk but I could tell that he saw me. I explained why I was there and told him I would be visiting with him weekly.

When I returned the next week, there was marked improvement in his ability to talk. He still couldn't do much else but when I asked him if he wanted me to read to him he responded by asking me if I played chess.

"Well, I know the rules," I said, "but I have only played a little so I am probably not very good."

"Would you try?" he said.

I nodded, and the next week I brought a set from home and played with him. This continued, and in fact I added another night of volunteering there so that one evening would be spent only with him.

During our playing, we talked a little about ourselves. I learned that he was born in Pennsylvania. He still had family there and was waiting for them to visit any day. He was single, and I guessed his age was close to mine. While he was not necessarily good looking, he was not homely, either. When I saw him finally standing, he appeared tall and somewhat stocky.

In the beginning of our chess playing he was propped up in his bed and I sat beside him so that we could play on the portable food tray. This routine lasted for months, and each time I saw him he was getting better.

Then one day, he told me he was being discharged and although he still needed therapy he was happy to be going back to his apartment. I maintained my one night a week slot, talking to the patients and handing out juice.

On one of those nights, the same nurse surprised me when she asked if I realized that I had saved the doctor's life.

"How do you think I did that?"

"Those visits meant everything to him," she said, "as you gave him strength to want to get better each day so that he could play chess with you."

I didn't know what to say.

"My guess is, that he has fallen for you!"

"Oh my," I said. "Now what do I do?"

I was already dating someone but I asked the doctor to join my family for Thanksgiving since I knew that he didn't have any plans. He was grateful for the invitation though my then boyfriend was furious.

After that somewhat awkward dinner, the doctor would occasionally call me to chat and advise me on how he was doing. I think that after awhile he had worked it out that I was not encouraging a relationship with him.

After some more months passed, he called to say he was moving to California. I felt badly about this but I simply did not know what to do or say.

We exchanged Christmas cards for many years. I knew he met and married a nurse and they adopted two children.

Then one day, he called to say he was coming to New York and would like to visit me with his wife. I was so pleased and looked forward to welcoming both of them to my apartment, where we all hugged in earnest.

"This is the lady I told you about who saved my life!"

he said to his wife.

He proudly showed me the only remaining "scar" from his accident—a limp in one foot, which required that he wear a leg brace for the rest of his life. But he was so happy to be almost back to normal. I do not recall his original medical specialty but I know he had to change it to something that allowed him to sit down while he worked.

Although this story had a happy ending for the good doctor I am saddened by the fact that after many years the Christmas cards stopped coming and I no longer remember his name.

## An Afghan Girl

I have served juice and talked with patients at the Veterans Administration hospital on 23rd Street. I've recorded blood pressure at the Hospital for Special Surgery. I've served on my building's condominium board for years. I even have a "100 Hours" certificate as an ombudsman for patients in a home for the aged. I love cats. Maybe I'll sign up to become a caregiver and rescue them.

My volunteer work continues with every new possibility that peaks my interest, and while this has opened up many positive opportunities, I have never felt the desire to participate in a cause I believe in. For example, I have never marched, hung out or tweeted on any subject, even when I have a strong opinion.

I think my strongest opinions are against rape—of women, and even worse, of children. It really disgusts me that in some cultures men still get away with rape despite laws forbidding it.

A few years ago, a story in the news called to me to do something I'd never done before. One morning, I read an article on the front page of *The New York Times* about an Afghan girl who was six years old. Her father had borrowed money to pay for medical expenses for his wife and his other children. The total amount of this loan was equal to $2,500 in U.S. currency.

The story went on to describe how under an unofficial Afghan system the man loaning the money had stated that if the sum were not paid within one year the six-year- old daughter of the borrower would be pledged to marry the 17-year-old son of the man who made the loan. The girl's father was worried that if she were ever mistreated it would be left to him to kill the young husband.

I was very moved by this story especially as it involved money used for medical expenses and the potential of a horrible future for this little girl. Normally, I do not look for causes. I give what I can to certain charities, like the U.S. Olympic committee, Smile Train (to fix cleft palates in poor children), Doctors Without Borders, North Shore Animal League, various museums and other organizations.

However, this particular case was begging for action.

As soon as I finished reading the article I went online, found an email contact for the writer and wrote that I would like to pay the $2,500 to the man who loaned the money. I explained that while I wanted anonymity I did want it to be known that the money had come from an American. I took a breath and pressed the send button.

The very next day, I saw a surprising headline on page A6 of the *Times*.

"Afghan Who Agreed to Trade His Daughter to End a Debt Says It Was Paid."

I knew this couldn't be me. Part of the story was

repeated but then the article went on about an American lawyer who had facilitated the payment in early March for an unnamed American who had also insisted to remain anonymous.

Apparently the reason this first article did not mention the payment was because the father of the girl wanted to respect the donor's wishes so he never mentioned the payment. However, when he heard that an article appeared about his predicament he made a call and confirmed that the payment indeed had been made.

Some further research revealed that while there is a judicial system in Afghanistan a tribal system also exists where elders make decisions by consensus. This is called a "jirga" and is particularly popular among the Pashtun people and other ethnic groups. The basis for a jirga is apparently the Quran, which commands consultation.

While considering how to handle the repayment, the American lawyer was concerned that the man who loaned the money would take it but not acknowledge later that it was in payment of a loan, and would insist that the daughter of the borrower must still wed the loaner's son. Furthermore, she worried that the borrower might use the money for his own purposes and not consider it the repayment of the debt. The lawyer wondered which would be more effective: a court order or a jirga. She decided that the jirga would be more respected among the people in this particular Pashtun clan so she arranged that the payment be made through the jirga system.

She was given the very unusual right of acting as the chairwoman—instead of one of the elders. Local mullahs were invited, as well as elders and witnesses from both sides. She personally handed the money to the man who loaned it. She obtained signatures of both sides by way of thumbprints since the borrower could neither read nor write. Given the situation, she felt that she had done as well as she could.

The journalist at the *Times* asked a professor at a university in Afghanistan whether he thought what she did would work. He responded that "there's no guarantee that two years from now the lender won't show up with a bunch of armed men and take the girl. Since the foundation of the agreement is unofficial, then everything is unofficial."

Afghanistan has an "Elimination of Violence Against Women" law but it has been difficult to enforce. And though it is illegal under Afghan national law, child marriage is unfortunately not uncommon.

I never received a response from the *Times* but I think they would assume that I read the second article and saw that the loan had been repaid. I hope this will have a good ending. Maybe the *Times* will report again on this story!

This reminds me of the story of a five-year-old Indian girl who was recently abducted, raped and tortured by a neighbor in New Delhi. This occurred shortly after a Swiss woman and her husband were victims of a robbery in India, and when it became clear that the amount robbed was low the men returned and raped the woman. The outpouring of rage against these incidents doesn't seem to have stopped these kinds of acts from repeating themselves.

According to *The New York Times*, "the number of rapes in the city (New Delhi) had more than doubled since December and cases of molesting had risen sixfold."

Maybe I should give that $2,500 to Human Rights Watch. At least it will be doing something!

## "Gorgeous"

New York Cares is an organization that utilizes volunteers to assist in a variety of projects that help those in need. One program brings people together on Saturdays each October to go into a public school to decorate or organize an upcoming event. Schools are invited to make a request and New York Cares coordinates a large number of volunteers for this annual program.

A few years ago, while looking for an interesting opportunity to volunteer, I saw a New York Cares ad on TV and contacted them to become a part of this public school program. On the designated day, I met up with a group and boarded a bus that took us to our respective schools. I was headed to Queens but I had no idea what the work would be. All I knew was that there were seven of us about to find out.

One project turned out to be organizing the school's library and the other was to paint a mural on the auditorium walls. I opted to join the painting group and our job was to fill in the outline that a volunteer artist had already drawn of various figures and animals. After being greeted by the school's administrative staff, who were quite excited to see us, we were given a short tour of the school before being led to the auditorium, where paint, brushes and rags had already been delivered.

The outlines covering one of the high walls were so clear that it was easy to apply the paint and not cross over any of the outlines. Hours went by easily as we painted and chatted together. By late in the day the wall came alive, revealing a large mural we had surprisingly turned from all gray into a beautiful blend of magnificent colors.

"Gorgeous," we all said.

The staff was thrilled and took photos and we were excited to imagine how the children would react the following Monday when they returned to school. Up until then, they were unaware this was going to happen. We eventually heard that the children loved the new look of their auditorium and their newly organized library.

I never felt the need to revisit the school. I was simply satisfied that our group had done this for the kids. In spite of the fact that I never joined the Peace Corps or volunteered downtown after 9/11, I like to do what I can now. For me, volunteer work has many positives. It keeps one busy and it's something good to do for others.

*A Great Train Ride*

I love trains. I don't know why, but the *chug-chug-chug* of a train on the tracks has always been a pleasant sound to me. From time to time, I've opted for train rides as a way to vacation. I took a three-week trip across Siberia in the 1980's. Besides the scenery and the comforting *chug-chug-chug*, I was surprised to be essentially unimpressed with the overall experience, especially because the private compartments were small and the food was practically inedible.

Years later, I flew to Albuquerque, New Mexico, to embark on a week-long train vacation visiting national parks in the western United States. As with the Siberian train, the size of the sleeping compartments was the first disappointment for just about all of us. During the first few moments viewing our quarters, many people ran to the train purser to pay extra money for larger quarters. There were only a few available and they were all purchased pretty swiftly.

My compartment was approximately three feet by six feet, which I think is smaller than a prison cell. It contained a sofa that became a bed and had a small sink with hardly any counter space to hold toiletries. The tiny bathroom only housed a commode and there was no bath or shower. If I wanted to take a shower, I had to make an appointment, so each morning at eight a.m. became my time slot.

I did not ask to change my room as the trip was expensive enough. I felt I simply had to work within this tiny environment and told myself I was lucky to have my own space. Sharing these quarters would have meant another bed would have fallen out of the wall above the couch.

Anyway, I kept my clothes and camera in my small suitcase, which barely fit under the couch. Unlike the amenities on a cruise ship, a train has no laundry, gym, pool or spa services. Nor can you walk the deck for exercise! There are no bridge games and there certainly is no theater for movies or live entertainment.

And one cannot learn dancing in a train car! Even walking from compartment to compartment could be risky if one had a difficult gait or walked with a cane. It was recommended that we wear supportive shoes when walking among the cars of the train.

In addition to the sleeping quarters for passengers and crew, there were two bar cars, two dining cars, one double-decker for lectures with a glass-domed ceiling for sightseeing, a car for the purser and his staff, another housing the kitchen and, finally, the engine car.

Each sleeping car had an assigned valet who provided early morning coffee or tea, which was especially nice on those mornings when I didn't want to go to the dining car but preferred having breakfast brought to my room.

Lunch was served as a buffet in one of the bar cars or you could choose the dining car for a more complete meal. Dinner was always in the dining cars. Most people went to a bar car for cocktails and then headed to the dining car for dinner. No matter what I ordered, it was always wonderful.

People on vacations are usually friendly. Most of the time, I approach a single woman to make a connection and then the two of us pick out two others to make up a table of four for dining together in the evenings. This has always worked for me and I am confident that it always will if I continue traveling alone.

When I take a tour off the train, I prefer viewing things on my own. I like listening to a guide or taking video so having someone with me can be a distraction. But I enjoy company at dinnertime.

I was curious about the kitchen facilities so I stopped by one day and asked for a tour. The staff was courteous and I wondered how they could possibly prepare the dishes they did in such incredibly narrow and crowded conditions.

I also asked if I could visit and perhaps ride with the train engineer in his car. To my delight, he said yes, but when I realized I would have to climb outside the train in order to enter the car I decided not to do it. A few months earlier I had broken my ankle and it still felt a bit weak so trying such a climb didn't feel like a good idea. I was disappointed because I knew I would never get a chance like that again unless I took another train journey.

But generally speaking, this train trip was a wonderful and unique experience, topped only by our tours off the train.

But that's another story...

*Condo Board Woes*

## Reconsidering the Board

I WAS ELECTED to my apartment building's Board of Managers seven years ago. We have 302 apartments, a property manager with an on-site office and a resident superintendent, supervising 17 employees.

The bylaws mandate that all twelve board members must run for office every year. This is unlike other buildings I know, where they have only nine positions and staggered terms. The notice to invite residents to run for the board is sent out every March and our annual meeting is held in April.

The following list describes what being a member of the board entails:

- *Attending monthly board meetings and occasional building meetings.*
- *Chairing and/or serving on a committee, as needed.*
- *Attending community meetings.*
- *Upholding the condominium's bylaws and governing documents.*

Three years ago, I was asked to consider taking on the role of board president. This came as a last-minute request from certain other members and though I accepted and subsequently received enough votes, I thought at the time that since I had served as chair for so many legal committees this new role would be similar.

However, as I read and re-read the condominium's bylaws, I realized that the president was responsible for running the entire building, from creating a budget to hiring staff through our property and resident managers. Therefore, I could not take sides concerning resident complaints, and would have to resolve problems while remaining neutral on whatever matter I was presiding over. This also meant that I couldn't—and wouldn't—take a position that favored one particular board member over another.

As I continued running the meetings, I was shocked with what I learned about the other board members, especially as it pertained to issues I hadn't focused on before. One member had a non-board member friend and would repeat confidential discussions and the voting breakdown from the meetings, both of which were highly unethical.

Another board member decided that the property manager and the resident super were managing the building in a fraudulent way by paying overtime to certain "favorite" employees. This member also used a particularly angry employee to obtain supposed evidence of the "crime."

The angry employee obtained purported evidence and handed it to the board member, who then argued to the board that the actions of management were clearly wrong. I created a committee, which eventually proved that there had been absolutely no mismanagement whatsoever.

This rogue board member never stopped arguing that she had a right to do what she did. My problem on this issue was the unethical way she went about her mission. It caused a serious rift in our previous friendly relationship, and for several years we didn't speak to each other, except during official exchanges at board meetings.

In another example of how things can be dysfunctional, a poorly fitted balcony door of another member kept the entire board and management occupied for several years arguing over who should pay to fix the problem.

During yet another disagreement, another board member never revealed a conflict of interest when the member brought an issue to the board and recommended how it should be handled.

*Ugh!*

Have I given you a taste of how frustrating all of this can be?

Very few members of the board adhered to the expectations of what membership is supposed to entail. Some were lazy about coming to meetings. Others agreed to be on a committee, but then became mysteriously unavailable for meetings. Getting the secretary to provide a draft of the minutes on time was just too much to ask. I couldn't get management to provide their reports until the day of the board meetings.

In the spring of 2014, I ended my third year as president. I am giving serious thought to walking away from the board despite the fact that residents approach me to say I am doing a very good job. Little do they know what I have endured.

*The Arabian Gulf*

If I'd have taken a trip to the Middle East 50 years ago, I would have found endless deserts, huts made of wood, intensive heat and small cities settled by various tribes of Bedouins. Over many decades, descendants of these tribes have expanded their lineage, avoided conflict and expanded their financial potential through intermarriage. For example, Osama bin Laden's father married multiple times so that he would have greater opportunities to secure building contracts, which is how he made his money, offering more proof that his marriages gave him an edge in his construction business.

But I didn't visit this intriguing part of the world 50 years ago. I traveled there in 2009 and found that oil has made a huge difference in the lifestyle of that region. In each country, proceeds have gone directly to the families with political power and it's been up to these sheiks and rulers—also known as benevolent dictators—to decide how they want to spend it.

In Dubai, the money from oil profits has been spent on building the biggest structures possible, many on land reclaimed from the gulf, including hotels, offices, residential buildings or malls, one of which features an indoor ski slope. The people in power hired the best architects and the new buildings built over the last decade or two offer a stunning vision of the city landscape. In fact, the tallest building in the world, designed by a firm in Chicago, just opened in Dubai.

When I arrived in Dubai, I learned that its ruler had simply overspent and now he could not pay his lenders, leaving the country in deep trouble. We subsequently heard that the ruler of Abu Dhabi would not let Dubai fall as these neighboring countries were connected through a couple of marriages and if Dubai's economy collapsed it would negatively impact other countries of the UAE. Supposedly, Dubai received a loan of 10 billion dollars from Abu Dhabi.

We also visited Sharjah, another UAE country whose ruler spent oil money on universities because he believes that education is paramount to anything else. We saw schools everywhere!

In Abu Dhabi, its ruler felt strongly that an emphasis on culture was the way to spend its oil money. He plans to build a Guggenheim museum, an opera house and a ballet theater, and he has paid dearly for the right to build a museum that will be called The Louvre. The French are in an uproar about this, asserting that an Arab country is not the place for another Louvre. The only one happy about any of this must be the director of the Louvre!

Besides the impressive modern buildings we saw in each of these countries, we also visited local mosques in each main city, as well as local markets, called "souks," where we enjoyed absolutely delicious local food.

Everyone (almost) speaks English and street signage was always in Arabic and English, which made it easy to get around and to buy things. The Arabs dress in long neck-to-ankle gowns, called a "dishdash." The men dress in white and the women in black in what they call an "abaya."

When the wind blew, one could see western garb under their garments, usually jeans. Some Arab women do not consider their black dress to be confining. Instead, they feel a kind of freedom in not having to dress nicely when they go out. They just throw on their abaya. We had to wear them in the mosques we visited as well as a black shawl that could cover all our hair.

One highlight of the trip was a visit to the Al Jazeera television station. I knew of the station from when the war against Iraq started and Al Jazeera was getting negative publicity because it aired taped messages from Bin Laden and showed photos of dead people that westerners felt were inappropriate. I had also seen a 2004 documentary called *The Control Room*, made by a film student who managed to get access to the station as well as to our soldiers, some of whom expressed dismay at fighting this war.

At the station, an American girl greeted us for our tour. She had been vacationing in the area four years earlier when she learned that the station had an open position on its English channel, which she applied for and secured. She totally believed that the station presents non-biased views. Al Jazeera also has an Arabic Channel, which the U.S. government monitors because they still believe that its programs are biased.

After a tour of both facilities, we met the general manager and communications director of the English Channel. I asked them about that 2004 documentary. Their response was that if they had known the level of distribution the film would receive they would have given the filmmaker even more access because they had been looking for a way to publicize the station.

We were also told that Al Jazeera has bureaus in London, Kuala Lumpur and Washington, D.C. They are anxious to bring this channel to the States. It is already available on the internet and much to our surprise, we discovered that Al Jazeera is available in a town in Vermont and another in Ohio because local people in both towns asked for it from their cable providers.

I was also fascinated by a special trip we made to a navy base in Doha, Qatar. Since we had a retired ambassador and his wife on our trip we were treated to places that no ordinary tourist could go. We were led in to the "War Room" and given a "non-classified" briefing about navy operations. It was interesting to hear how our navy protects the waters in the gulf and how the Straits of Hormuz is in a vulnerable spot where pirates can hide and jump out at passing ships. In fact, the week before we embarked on our cruise ship, it had been approached by pirates but our captain was able to get them to leave by holding them at bay with water hoses and placing electric wiring around the ship in strategic places.

After visiting Bahrain and Oman, our final highlight was having tea with the ruler of Raz Al Khamai, another Emirate. At his palace, we were led into a large reception room where we waited for him to enter and have tea with us. We had been given a lecture about our manners, etiquette, how to sit and how to drink tea. We already knew what to wear and the women were covered from wrists to ankles. The ruler shook hands with each of us and asked random questions. When it was my turn, he noticed my nametag revealed that I was a graduate of Columbia University. He animatedly pointed that out and said that he had someone on his staff who was also a graduate. He himself had degrees from the University of Michigan and spoke English very well and I was almost embarrassed that I was the only one in the group he seemed to really relate to.

I must also mention the beautiful scenery outside of the cities, especially the deserts and mountains (and camels). And I can't leave out the three lunch dates we had with the current American ambassador in those countries, courtesy of the retired ambassador in our group who arranged these wonderful visits. It's hard to imagine any future trip that could top this experience.

But that's another story...

*Career*

## Breaking Barriers?!

NO ONE TOLD ME that if I became a lawyer I would suffer discrimination. I didn't notice this possibility in 1959 when I was the only female in my law school class of 100 students, and I didn't see it coming when one semester I received higher grades than three of my male friends in the class, which prompted them to stop speaking to me for the next several months!

So after three years of grueling concentration, I graduated with a law degree, took and passed the bar exam on my first try and received my license to practice law.

Time to start looking for a job. I responded to ads placed in the Tuesday edition of *The Wall Street Journal* and always received an appointment for an interview. On these occasions, I would be asked if I could type (I could) and if I would be agreeable to sitting at a secretarial station instead of in an office of my own. The salary these places offered did not even cover my transportation costs to and from the office. One interviewer even said that while it was company policy not to hire women lawyers he was "curious" to see what I was like!

I finally accepted a non-legal position, which the company preferred filling with qualified lawyers. Luckily, a couple ran the company and the wife hired me. I stayed six months and left because it *was* a non-legal position.

I traveled to Europe. When I arrived in London nearing the end of my trip, I decided to see what might be available there. I took a job that a lawyer would do even though my degree was not recognized in that country. After two years, I returned home and much to my delight a law had been passed that forbade discrimination on several fronts. A company in Michigan desperate for another attorney offered me a position, which I accepted. Although I loved the job, I hated the small "company town" environment, so I quit and moved back to New York.

My first position in New York was with the same company that had previously told me it was their policy not to hire women lawyers. Now I was their first and I had an actual office, but none of the male lawyers would befriend me, except one. I stayed in that position for only two years since the legal work was confined to U.S. law and I wanted to branch out to do international law.

I found what I thought was a desirable position in another company where I was also their first female attorney. After a few years, I concluded that I had been hired because my male boss figured that promoting me would be unnecessary and unlikely. Even worse, several years went by without a salary increase because I wouldn't respond to the attentions of a married male lawyer who was responsible for all our salaries.

Nevertheless, I stayed with that company for 19 years!

# Gender Gap

In 1969, I accepted a position as a trademark attorney with a large corporation. As the first female lawyer to be hired by the company, I reported to a man named Rich, who told me I had been hired because—according to him—I had the experience he needed. That was encouraging, at least until I was shown to a small office far away from anyone else, where it seemed like if they could get away with hiding me, they would.

I was kept very busy from day one so it took some time before I saw how this department was really being run. Rich was out to make himself a major department head. Since trademarks and patents were very important to this company, our department was likely to become a large priority and a major asset moving forward.

Rich created some interesting strategies for this buildup. He would never answer a question directly. Instead, he would ask a question in return. Once that was answered, he would pose another. This would go on for weeks or months before any actual work on the matter would begin. Over the years, this "game" would result in a series of false impressions that our department needed more help, so Rich would invariably get permission to hire yet another lawyer for his department.

As I grew to understand what he was doing, I started to rebel. I thought that being hired to do a job meant that one should do it as efficiently as possible.

One year, Rich decided to tour the company's satellite offices, which were located all around the world. He got the permission from his higher-ups and off he went, leaving me to handle the day-to-day operations.

I did not follow Rich's practice of answering questions

with more questions, leading to an endless spiral of inactivity. Under my watch, each question put to the department was handled immediately. I also created a form that made it easier for the marketing people to pose the right questions and to give us instructions about obtaining trademark rights around the world. The marketing people loved what I had done.

Rich returned from his trip, noted the changes I had initiated and made it clear that he did not like them at all. He could not do anything about it because everything was already in place and he couldn't argue the fact that it was an efficient system.

But he could do something about me.

From that time on, Rich became critical. Whenever he managed to hire other lawyers for the department, he made sure that they were given perks that I was not.

He even sent me to Japan on a mission to solve a rather knotty legal problem that our lawyers originally counseled was something we could not do. Rich was shocked when I returned home victorious.

When I took a Swedish company to court in Sweden over trademark infringement, Rich told people in the company that I would win even though he really thought I would lose. In fact, I discovered later that he was hoping that if I did not win the case it would reverberate badly on me, and my position at the company.

I know he was shocked when I won the case!

With all of these events happening one after the other, the emotional stress was taking its toll on me. I wanted to leave the company, but my mother kept reminding me that I was "lucky to have a job." Regrettably, I held on to my position for many years.

That's when I received an offer to become department

head—not simply another staff attorney—at another company. Announcing this news gave me such a joyful feeling. But after a year at this new position I left and joined a law firm.

I learned a very important lesson during this time that corporate positions are not about doing a good job. They are about making your boss look good to his or her boss!

So becoming my own boss years later was an exceptionally satisfying transition.

## Violation

I was in my thirties when I bought my one and only mink coat. I loved it.

One day, while walking home from my law firm along Third Avenue, a woman stopped me and asked if I knew that there was red paint on the back of my fur coat. She was kind enough to accompany me to a nearby coffee shop, where I took off the coat and looked at the back. She was right. Someone had literally poured red paint all over it!

The woman said she saw the person who did this duck into an open door of another shop. I decided not to go after her but walked to the closest police precinct and showed them what had happened. The look of indifference I received was disappointing, even though I had to admit that the police had far more serious issues to deal with than my mink coat.

I walked the rest of the way to my apartment and with each step I became more and more agitated. I felt violated and couldn't get the incident out of my mind. I learned the next day that Joan Rivers had also been a victim of the same act and the newspapers carried her rant against PETA, who denied the allegation.

Days later, I took the coat to my furrier with instructions to clean it and turn it into a raincoat with the remaining fur to be placed on the inside of the coat. This meant that the fur would be sheared so that it could be used as a lining and a waterproof material could be put over it so that my former mink would function as a raincoat.

They did a great job and I still wear the coat, but I know I'll never buy another one again made from any kind of fur.

## My Almost Second Career

I have always appreciated movies and the editing process that goes into making them. So I welcomed the chance to assist my nephew in editing a piece he wrote, directed and filmed for a project in his Boston film school, In fact, the experience was so enjoyable I signed up to study film at NYU's school of continuing education as soon as I returned home. Their certificate program consisted of about nine courses held at night. Due to my busy workload as a lawyer, I took only one course a semester.

During this period, I grew to appreciate documentary films more than fiction. I even had thoughts of leaving law and making films as a new career. When I received my Certificate in Film in 1997, I began taking more courses specifically concerned with the making of a documentary. I noted that few filmmakers who made documentaries made any kind of real money for their efforts. Most people financed their work with personal credit cards, which I considered financially inappropriate.

I also realized that I almost did not care enough about any particular cause that would have me leave my legal position, do the necessary research, make the film on my credit card and beg local art theaters to show it. As a result, for a time I simply went to see films of friends who did use credit cards and got local theaters to show them.

But I continued taking a course or two on documentary filmmaking. In one class, a fellow student named Janet approached me with an idea about making a documentary about a program offered each summer at Yale University for women who want to enter public service. Courses covered topics such as how to campaign, how to deal with the media and how to cope with unexpected problems that arise during a campaign.

Janet asked me to edit her piece. She had already interviewed a cinematographer whom she would have to pay but she could not afford anyone else. Since I was already on salary as a lawyer, I offered to do it for free and expected to enjoy the experience.

I rushed to take an intensive two-weekend course on the Avid, which at the time was considered to be state-of-the-art computerized editing software. NYU did not yet have these machines, as they cost about $80,000 each. Editing there was still being done under the old manual system, as it had been for more than 50 years, which made it a very arduous task. Luckily, Janet also agreed to pay for the cost of renting the Avid studio.

That summer, we went to Yale for a week and Janet guided the cinematographer about what and where to shoot. She then turned the tapes over to me to start editing in the Avid studio. I took a week off as vacation and spent it working my new "second career."

Unfortunately, Janet was not pleased with how the story was presented even though we had agreed on this aspect. But I had to return to my normal work and couldn't spend any more time on the film. Janet found someone else to complete the editing and her husband worked hard to get it shown that year on a PBS station. It was called *See Jane Run* and I was thrilled to see my name included in the screen credits.

Soon after, I signed up for a course at the New School called History of the Documentary. One day, our lecturer announced that she had 50 hours of film she had shot about her brother who had been taken away by the State when he was young to live in a home for the mentally impaired. Doctors had persuaded her parents at the time that this was the right thing to do. Susan's parents never told her what happened to her brother. All she remembered was that at the age of nine her brother was gone one day—never to return. Occasionally, when she was a bit older and her parents thought she could handle it, Susan accompanied her parents to visit her brother. He never spoke. He just made strange noises so being with him, according to Susan, was a strain.

Susan's interest in filmmaking grew over the years and she recently came to the conclusion that she wanted to tell the story of her brother through this medium. One day in class, she asked if any of us had time to help her categorize the footage she had shot, to determine the content of each scene and whether it was technically usable.

I volunteered and we agreed to meet at her house in Brooklyn so that I could see some of the footage. The only thing I knew about Brooklyn was Coney Island, the Brooklyn Academy of Music and the building in Brooklyn Heights where the Brooklyn Law School was located when

I went there. Although Susan told me what trains to take, I was not totally comfortable traveling there. I joked about this with Susan.

"Brooklynites consider New York City just a train stop away," she said, "but Cityites think Brooklyn is a country away!"

I had to agree. But I did go and before I was finished with the project I had gone there many times. When Susan realized that she wanted to film more scenes, I joined her for a trip upstate to visit the hospital where her brother had been, and then we visited her brother in a home where he had eventually been placed.

It took several months to complete the work Susan wanted. She went on to hire an editor, whom she fired, and then another editor, and there was a third person, as well.

Directors and editors sometimes have a hard time with each other when they approach the work with very different ideas about what should be done. A director becomes so involved with the piece while an editor is more logical and less emotional. It can be a contest of passion versus pragmatism.

Anyway, my part was done. Many months later, when Susan announced that the film was completed, she told me that the work I had done was extremely helpful in putting the piece together. She called it *Without Apology*.

The first screening was at the offices of the Association of Retarded People in upstate New York. Most of the people in the audience had a sibling in the system. When the first scene came on the screen I was thrilled because it was a scene I had shot with Susan's camera. This was in addition to the work I had put in during the pre-editing phase, and I saw that she had given me several screen credits.

Susan sent the film off to documentary film festivals and won quite a few accolades. The Two Boots theater on the lower east side of New York had a screening one night, which I attended. Years later, I went to another screening during a conference at Columbia University where Susan spoke and showed the film.

It's been a long time now since I've done any further film work. Janet left the city and never did another film. Susan continues teaching and making documentaries and she visits her brother regularly.

I've never done anything further because I still haven't found a subject I feel passionate enough about to risk maxing out my credit cards. However, I did video my godchild's wedding in a castle in Ireland, which I edited and gave to him. I also put together a film piece about my niece and her fiancé, which was shown at a party before their wedding. Hopefully, one of these days I will find the time and motivation to edit all my travel videos, which have now accumulated into quite a sizeable pile.

## Expanding My Resume

Though not exactly toys, I do like collecting certificates of completion. But of course it's not the gold-embossed paperwork I'm after; it's what each of these certificates represent in terms of learning!

For example, I have always had an interest in movies. I like to study how they are made. As a young adult, when my nephew and I would indulge in watching movie marathons on weekends, we would sit in a coffee shop and talk about all the different aspects of the film—the music, the acting, the script and the editing. My particular appreciation for the editing process led me to garnering an actual certificate from NYU.

But my certificate collection did not end there.

During the years I spent working as a corporate lawyer, I was asked to speak to various audiences on my area of practice. In 1984 and 1988, I was presented with award certificates for speaking or chairing a committee.

In the personal arena, my interest in caregiving resulted in a "100 Hours of Service" certificate from a hospital where I volunteered many years ago.

In 2003, I took a 20-hour intensive training in preparation for working in a hospice. That resulted in a certificate of completion even though I never got to do any hospice work. Maybe someday I will.

In 2005, I took a three-month course offered by the New York State Office for the Aging to become a patient advocate for those individuals living in nursing homes. In this case, I found ample time to give the organization a year of work as an ombudsman at a nursing home in Washington Heights.

I have always been interested in non-medical ways to reduce stress as I have had elevated blood pressure most of my life. I have studied many subjects, like meditation, acupuncture and Reiki, with its three levels of study. I completed the first level and have used what I learned to practice on myself. I have even studied French several times and have always wanted to speak fluently. If there were a certificate for speaking French fluently, I would pursue it.

There is so much to learn and I intend to keep going!

*Rosh Hashanah 5771*

As someone raised Catholic, attending a synagogue for the first time seemed like traveling to a foreign country.

Back in 2010, my neighbors invited me to Rosh Hashanah services at the conservative temple B'nai Jeshurun on West 88th Street. I had been inside a synagogue before but this was the first time during such a major holiday with so many people and I had no idea what to expect. The trip was just a few blocks away, and as soon as we entered, I noted the beautiful design and the organ pipes.

*Oh good, there will be organ music.*

Much to the surprise of my friends, the service started on time at 6:30 p.m. They were surprised because according to them, nothing done by Jews for Jews ever starts on time. The service began with chanting, which continued for most of the next hour and was accompanied by several musicians playing instruments, including a cello.

I tried to figure out what I was hearing because I had never heard such tones before. In one respect, after hearing a part of a chant repeated I could almost sing along, but in another respect it was complex—and also in Hebrew—so I couldn't understand a word. But most of the congregants knew every word and note and when it came time to sing together, they did so easily and wholeheartedly, and the music being in a minor key made it sound so soulful and beautiful. One doesn't have to be Jewish to appreciate this!

I had no idea that the next ten days were holy days, culminating in a Yom Kippur service in venues all over the city, especially in my general neighborhood, where one could hear this splendid music everywhere. Perhaps I will go with my friends to this service sometime.

But that's another story...

*Relationships*

## Marriage...?

RELATIONSHIPS ARE COMPLICATED. My experience with men, in particular, has generally not been successful. Starting early on, my sister and I grew up enjoying quality time with my father only on Sunday mornings when he would play Gilbert and Sullivan on our record player and we would memorize the lines. But that was all.

Growing up from then on, for one reason or another, I encountered an unfortunate string of unavailable men. This occurred despite the fact that I turned down three different marriage proposals. In fact, I ended up feeling grateful each time I backed out before it was too late, knowing that things would not have worked. That intuition became my saving grace.

These relationships were hard for me because the men were not emotionally available—something I was all too used to from my childhood—but ultimately not conducive to a good relationship.

Then there was Paul.

I have never been a hard liquor person but I spent many

nights downing martinis to ease the pain of losing Paul.

Paul was not my first boyfriend—nor would he be my last—but he was the love of my life! I was in my 30's when we met at the company where we were both working as attorneys. Paul had graduated from Harvard Law School and spent time in Venezuela as a Rhodes scholar. He was quite good looking and smart and our mutual love for the ballet is what brought us together.

Our relationship began during a company outing at a resort in Pennsylvania. Unbeknown to each other, we had both signed up to go horseback riding and we introduced ourselves and made general conversation. When we returned to New York City, Paul called me and we started seeing each other. We spent much of our time together going to the ballet—any ballet—both famous companies and unknown ones.

It didn't take long before it seemed natural for us to move in together, so we did. My apartment was the closest to our office so Paul moved in with me. He had told me early on about his marriage to a nationally known ballet choreographer in Caracas whom he met there during his Rhodes scholarship. He told me that when she became pregnant, though he was stunned by her announcement, he married her there. Back in those days (and maybe even now) you could get married in Venezuela simply by signing at a registry. No pomp, no vows, no ceremony—just signatures. And this is what they did.

Although Paul loved his newborn son, the marriage went downhill. Paul decided that a return to New York with his wife and son might make a positive difference in their life, but apparently it didn't so Paul sent his wife and son back to Venezuela.

When I learned about this marriage, I felt badly for

Paul, as he was saddened by how things had worked out. But I felt quite comfortable that it was over for him, and I knew that I had nothing to do with his marriage breaking up. So staying in our relationship seemed like a good idea at the time and we continued on our way.

Paul's job required that he travel to South America a couple of times a year. When he came back from one of his trips he told me that he had started divorce proceedings and after subsequent trips he updated me on the status of the proceedings.

Then, during our second year together, Paul was offered an opportunity that completely changed our lives. Our company asked him to go to Rome to work out of their office there. Paul wanted to accept the position, as it represented a considerable promotion. He asked me to quit my job and go with him. I didn't speak Italian and was afraid that getting hired as an attorney in Italy—especially in those days—would be difficult, but I agreed to go with him if the company would transfer me, too.

My request was denied because the kind of law I practiced, though international, was handled only out of the New York office. I told Paul I was too uncomfortable to take the chance of finding work in Italy and I didn't want to rely on him to support me if I ended up being there without any work.

When the day came for Paul to fly to Rome, I drove out to JFK to see him off. Neither of us talked about the future. We both thought we just had to see what would happen. After two weeks in Rome, Paul called me and said that he missed me too much. Then he proposed. I immediately said yes, as I was in love with him, though still very much conflicted about leaving the U.S. and making a life in Italy.

Then he said that he had one thing to take care of before we talked further about getting married, and that was to transfer his divorce proceedings to New York if he was ever going to get a divorce. To that end, he needed to find a New York divorce lawyer and asked me if I would find one. Despite feeling awkward about the whole situation, I got a recommendation and made an appointment.

I told the divorce attorney that I needed to know how to transfer an ongoing proceeding in a foreign country so that the proceedings could continue in New York. He said that he needed to know the court where the action was pending and the serial numbers of Paul's case so that he could obtain copies and file the necessary documents for a transfer.

I called Paul to tell him what we needed to do.

"Okay!" he said.

Then came a long pause before he continued.

"There is something that I have to tell you. I never started any divorce proceedings. I want to do that now."

I was absolutely shocked by this revelation. I thought back to all the stories I had been told each time he returned from a trip to South America.

"Why did you lie so much to me?"

"I worried that you would end our relationship if you knew the truth."

I hung up totally exhausted from the conversation. I spent hours, days and weeks crying over this and drowning my sorrows in martinis. After about a month, I wrote to him and said that he was right—our relationship was over. I couldn't trust him, and since that was the case, I obviously couldn't marry him, either.

My mother had met Paul and liked him. What mother wouldn't? He was intelligent, good looking, easy going and a Harvard trained lawyer. So when I told her about Paul's chronic lying she was very disappointed and even suggested I should simply forgive him. I don't think she considered the possibility that I might be giving up a career, let alone trying to make a life with a man who was not altogether honest.

It took me a year before I was able to resume my life without feeling depressed.

Four years later, I was still at our company but Paul had left the company while still in Rome and remained there for another two years. Meanwhile, his Italian became fluent and he took up with a woman there and worked with her in some sort of business.

One Saturday morning, my phone rang. It was Paul, who had just arrived in New York from Rome. He wanted to come over, and for some reason, I agreed.

As soon as I opened the door and our eyes met we were both in tears. We just sat on my couch for a long time, crying. Paul told me he still hadn't gotten the divorce because it had taken him so long to even admit to himself that he had actually gotten married in the first place. Therefore, since he couldn't come to terms with having done that, the idea of divorce seemed unreal.

That was a lot for me to digest.

A few hours later, he left, saying he would call again when he resettled somewhere. After eventually being hired for a legal position in Louisiana, he asked if I would visit him. I went to Baton Rouge several times and he also visited me repeatedly in New York. We tried hard to make "us" work again but it was not to be. Too much time had passed and we had grown into different people than who we had been for the two years we spent together. The trips back and forth stopped. I started dating someone else and he did, too.

One day, Paul called out of the blue to say that he and

his wife (he had finally divorced and remarried) were moving to Libya. He was a little concerned about going there, but it was a good promotion.

When he called to tell me of this new venture, Paul announced that he had a question for me.

"Did you ever really love me?" he said.

"Paul, you were the love of my life!"

"Okay," he said. "I have to board now."

That was it. I said goodbye, we hung up and I never heard from him again!

Sometimes, when I think back on that relationship, I remember an incident involving Paul's questionable behavior. Our company had a requirement that their lawyers be members of at least one state bar. The company would hire you prior to taking the exam, but you were expected to pass it. However, after Paul was hired he did not pass the bar exam and never told the company. They found out somehow when Paul left the Rome office. It was all very embarrassing for me because the company knew about us when I had asked for a transfer. So when this information about the bar came out, I had to sort of go into hiding until it died down.

I have no idea why Paul thought that I might not have cared about him. Perhaps it was because I hadn't rushed to be with him in Rome. I sometimes think that my career may have been more important to me than marriage. After all, Paul was the second proposal I turned down.

In the 1970's, women felt that the cut-off date for bearing a child was around 40. I was one of those women. At age 38, I was not yet married, and since I had rejected the option twice already by then I thought there was no prospect for me at the time.

I felt very ambivalent about marriage and children. The

part of me that wanted both came about because in those days that was what most women were seeking. Even though I was a practicing attorney with a full-time career and could have married my job, I still felt pangs of concern, as if I may be missing something fundamental in life.

Then I started dating Al, who was not a lawyer but a doctor, a dermatologist. Our relationship was great at first, as we both liked the arts and went to many concerts, films and plays. We even spent our first summer at his country cottage, learning how to count in blackjack. By the end of August, we both had two decks and four decks committed to memory, anticipating of course that we would beat the house. We decided it was time for a trip to Las Vegas, where we spent one evening winning—not a great deal but a fairly tidy sum for all our effort.

But soon after, I began noticing that he could be very controlling and critical. Even so, my internal clock was ticking and I tried to make the relationship work by focusing on the enjoyment of doing things together that we liked.

About a year later, the subject of marriage and children came up.

"While I want children," he said, "I only want one son. If you get pregnant, you have to take a test, and if it's a girl you have to agree to have an abortion."

I remember exactly where I was when we had this discussion. We were standing on line, waiting to go into a movie theater. I was shocked at the matter-of-factness of his request and I think my interest in marrying started to wane right then. But it didn't completely end right then and there because I thought I could work on changing his attitude. That is how much the ticking clock was getting hold of me.

Our relationship continued, but a trip to Europe became stressful because he prepared a very complicated agenda, which made the whole thing terribly hectic and tiring. After that trip, the relationship ended.

I noticed that my ambivalence was gone. A weight had been lifted off my shoulders. I felt as if I had my freedom back. Although I continued to date and had one very long-term relationship, I did not marry and never had children.

## *Where Were You On 9/11?*

I woke up to a typical workday on September 11, 2001. I had an appointment in Danbury, Connecticut, with the general counsel of a client company. I usually made this trip once a year to discuss pending matters. I would take the train from Grand Central to Brewster, New York, and get a taxi to Danbury for the 15-minute drive to the client. I usually arrived by 10:30 a.m. and would meet with the lawyer before having lunch in the company's cafeteria and heading back to New York City via taxi and train. This was a simple routine for several years.

On that day, now 15 years ago, things started out normally. I left my home on the Upper East Side to catch an 8:44 train, which left on time and was proceeding quite unremarkably until a lot of cell phones started ringing as we headed north of the city.

Those who answered didn't stay on long and turned to those of us who were not using cell phones and yelled that there had been an "occurrence" at the World Trade Center when a plane hit one of the buildings. I immediately remembered an incident from my childhood when a plane hit the Empire State building so I thought this must be another terrible accident like that.

A few minutes later, cell phones started ringing again. Another plane had hit the World Trade Center. I immediately decided that this was not an accident but must be something deliberate. I felt I should stay on the train because being away from the city seemed to be a safer option.

When I arrived at my client's company, no one was working. The receptionist told me that everybody in the building was huddled in a big conference room where the BBC was being shown on a large screen TV. As I turned to make my way there, the receptionist said that I probably wouldn't get back to the city that day so she was making a hotel reservation for me. I thanked her for thinking ahead like that even though I had no idea until later how grateful I would be for her foresight.

As I was headed to the conference room, I saw a phone on a table and called my sister at her business in New Jersey. She was very glad to hear that I was okay and to learn where I was, as she had not known what to think when she first heard the news.

Our annual business meeting never took place. No one could think. We just watched the BBC's coverage of the events on TV. Everyone was shocked, unable to believe what they were seeing. I stayed a while and then went to the hotel, knowing that all modes of transportation had been suspended in and out of the city.

I don't know how I managed through the night, but when you're in shock things happen almost by themselves.

The next morning, I tried calling to ask if the trains were running but I could not get through so I took my chances and caught a taxi to the train station. One actually came and I returned to Grand Central.

I will never forget how quiet the city was. No one was walking fast or hanging around or laughing. The serious look on most faces revealed how shocked everyone was, including me. We were all moving about in some kind of trance.

As soon as I got home I turned on the TV and heard that no one was allowed to go south of 14th Street. I was living on 59th Street at the time and planned to stay put.

The next day, I took a walk with a friend along 1st Avenue heading south. When we were close to Bellevue Hospital, the whole scene became very emotional. People had hung photos of missing loved ones any place they could. There were hundreds of them posted just across from the makeshift morgues that had been placed there and remained for a very long time.

That was my only venture on that day and it was quite enough.

On the following weekend, a niece arrived on what had been a preplanned visit. I told her that I would like to go down to the World Trade Center. She agreed and we took the train most of the way and walked the rest. It was before any security barriers had been put up so we had free access at the site.

What we saw was horrible. Everything—every parked car, every store window, every last thing—was covered in rubble and gray soot. We did not stay very long as I was convinced that the air quality was poor.

It annoyed me that the city's health department continued to claim that the air quality was fine. How could it have been? The news on television kept reporting about multiple first responders and volunteers but this was one volunteer position I decided not to pursue.

During the following days, I began to hear about people I knew.

There was a law firm located in one of the buildings that I had worked in at one time. Everyone there lost his or her life that morning.

The husband of a couple who lived in my apartment building worked for an investment house in one of the buildings and he died that day, too.

A former paralegal of mine who was working at a firm a couple of streets away ran all the way to 34th street when her firm realized what was happening.

I am very grateful that I did not lose anyone with whom I am close.

On the other hand, I am saddened to know that so many first responders, who spent days and days at the site and were subsequently diagnosed with lung cancer or other ailments, have been suffering ever since or have already died, leaving their families without their main breadwinner, husband and father. Most of their loved ones have been financially compensated—although who knows if it's enough—and if it could ever heal their loss.

But that's another story...

*Law School*

# What a Challenge!

MY MOTHER ALWAYS TOLD ME that I would make a good lawyer. I carried that thought around for years until I decided during my senior year in college to try law school. I had been wrestling with the idea of going to the London School of Economics for a graduate degree or McGill University in Canada. When I was accepted to Brooklyn Law School I decided to take the challenge because back in those days it was not common for women to go to law school or medical school or business school, either, for that matter.

I did not think of myself as opening new doors for women, nor did I suspect the prejudice I would face. I simply applied and was accepted for the fall semester of 1959.

On the first day of class I noted that I was the only female among 100 men, but luckily there was a women's lounge in the school because there were other women (maybe ten) in different classes and at different levels. I simply accepted the situation for what it was and gave little thought to being in such a minority.

I took three subjects the first semester: torts, contracts and administrative law. I had no idea what the professors were talking about and the concepts were very foreign to me. (Law school data reports that more than 30 percent of initial enrollees drop out during the first few months.) I had no relatives who were lawyers and had never had contact with one so I had no sense of what an attorney had to know in order to practice.

Up until that point, my only experience with the practice of law was a television show, called *Perry Mason,* but that show was basically about defending criminals, which is actually a very small part of practicing law. Every subject I had to take seemed like an advanced physics class being taught in a foreign language. I absolutely hated school and told myself every day that I could not go on. There was so much homework in the reading and analysis of case law!

I was told that the only way to learn all of this legal material and pass the tests was to join or create a study group. So I was really happy when a couple of male students invited me to join them, saving me the trouble of having to start my own and ask others to join. Our group of three males and I met once a week in school or at the apartment of one of us who lived nearby. We were all serious about learning the course work so our group functioned well for two years. My grades were mostly B's with an occasional C. I rarely got an A.

But during the second semester of my second year I received an A in a tax course. The boys got B's, which they took badly. They told me I would be taking a job that should really go to a man. Then they said that I should not be in law school at all. How dare I compete with the men!

Clearly it was going to be hard to maintain our study

group so it was quickly abandoned. Luckily, another man asked if I wanted to study with him. I said yes and we finished our third year together.

Those were the most focused three years of my life. They also exposed my split personality. On the one hand, I was determined to see it through and pass the bar exam so I could get a license to practice law. The other part of me was quiting every single day. To this day, I still don't know why that one part of me won out over the other.

I had no other life. I didn't go out socially and felt that all I should do was study. My mother, who waited on me all three years, helped me through this period. She wanted this for me and I knew it, so whenever I had those impulses to quit I would count how much longer I had to go and talk myself into staying.

After three solid years of morning classes, afternoons working for a professor to fulfill my working scholarship and evening and weekend studies, I graduated in June 1962. I did not receive any special awards though I heard I had been considered for the category of "most likely to succeed."

I spent the next six weeks hitting the books again to review all 21 courses I had taken in hopes of passing the July bar exam. I felt that I had to pass it the first time as I feared I would not try taking it a second time. I would just give it all up. So I asked my mother to visit my sister in another state so that I could stay in the house all day and night by myself with our dog and study. My only free time was to walk the dog. I had to review every class I had taken during the three years as separate legal topics that would be one two-day-long exam.

I was very lucky to be assigned to the new Fordham Law School at Lincoln Center. The classrooms were air-conditioned and very comfortable. I had heard some awful stories about being assigned to hot and dingy rooms in buildings that were not air-conditioned.

One of the women I had met in the women's lounge when I was a freshman said that in the essay sections of the exam it is best to write and write as much as you can because every correct sentence can become a point in my favor. So that is what I did.

When those two grueling days were over I couldn't wait to get home and go to sleep.

I had to wait until November to find out if I passed, which I did! In those days, the students names who passed were published in *The New York Times*. Someone had given me a phone number in Albany where if I got through I could ask a couple of days ahead of publication whether or not I had passed. Someone agreed to look up my name and after what seemed like forever she returned to the phone to tell me the good news. I thanked her for doing me the favor and then called my mother immediately. She was thrilled.

From that day on, I began looking for jobs and realized for the first time that there was real discrimination against women, a fact my mother certainly hadn't known about and I didn't recognize despite the way I had been treated in school.

Luckily, I have never had problems obtaining positions in my field and my work has given me opportunities to travel, which I love. Even though I was likely never paid what my male counterparts were, I can't complain about the life this career has given me.

The challenge of getting through law school was one of the hardest I ever undertook. I think it helped me deal with all sorts of other challenges throughout my life.

*Trouble in Taormina*

To say that Taormina, a town on the east coast of Sicily overlooking the Ionian Sea and the Mount Etna volcano, is picturesque would be an understatement. It is breathtakingly beautiful with its Greek and Roman architecture located along narrow, bustling streets.

I visited there in the late 70's with my boyfriend Al. After a week in Morocco we flew to Rome for a few days and then arrived in Taormina, Sicily's first resort, where we planned to stay for two nights in Hotel San Domenico Palace, which had originally been a monastery and still retained the beauty and peacefulness one imagines it originally had as a religious institution. We loved everything about the hotel, including the food. And when we ventured outside the grounds, we found a delightful town.

Al and I were in a very romantic mood on our last evening there. We had met about a year before and while we had a lot in common—our love of traveling being only one thing—I had some difficulty with his need to control the relationship, which even included what I wore. On the other hand, I was reaching a point in life where having children could become difficult if I waited much longer.

So there we were, far away from home, in a very comfortable mood. Over dinner in the hotel, Al proposed. In fact, he wanted to find a Catholic priest to marry us right then and there in Taormina. This surprised me because he was Jewish. I told him I would consider it but I would prefer getting married back home in the U.S.

I was still fighting with myself over the negatives of our relationship and the desire to have children. He kept trying to coax me into marrying him in Taormina by saying that marrying in such a beautiful location would be something we would always remember.

I kept telling him, "Let's talk about this when we are back in the States."

When he quieted down, I assumed that he was okay with my response. We were scheduled to leave the next day to spend three nights in Catania and then fly to Paris for two days before returning home. I was looking forward to the rest of our trip.

The hotel in Catania was fine but more like a big Hilton as opposed to the remarkable palace we had just left. Al and I chose to have dinner in the hotel. We were seated in the restaurant, about to order, when he suddenly got up and walked away without saying anything.

I had no idea how to respond, so I went to the lobby and headed to the elevator to go up to our room to see if he had gone there. When the elevator door opened, I saw Al standing inside with a knife in his hand pointing straight at me. I ran to the reception desk and told the staff. I asked for another room and requested that they not tell him where I was. I was given a key to another room and a staff member went to our original room and got my luggage. Luckily, we hadn't unpacked very much and I was able to describe exactly what was mine. Apparently, Al was not in the room and no one had seen him anywhere in the hotel after the incident in the elevator.

Who knows where he went? But I spent a very nervous night in my new room, shocked, of course, which was made all the more difficult because I was in a foreign country and didn't speak the language.

The next morning, the concierge told me that I had to move out. They simply did not want any trouble and they figured my presence—even though Al had not been seen again—might cause trouble. At least they called another hotel and booked me there for two more nights.

I spent the days walking around Catania, which was not too exciting because it was simply a big city with lots of car fumes and nothing in particular one would call attractive. I also had no idea if I would run into Al, and if I did, what would happen?

I checked out two days later and headed for the airport to fly to Paris. I had already decided to see if I could take the next plane from there back to New York.

Catania's airport was crowded and some Americans told me about a pilot strike delaying our flights. I sat with one couple for hours, waiting to see if the strike would end any time soon. At one point, I saw Al not far away. I had already told the couple my story and they said I would be crazy to approach him. I was a little nervous but I went up to him and although he looked a little strange he was polite. He did not indicate in any manner that he was pleased to see me but he was civil. I asked him where he had been. He told me only that he had checked himself into a hospital and that he now felt better.

*Really? About what?*

Then we all heard that one plane was about to take off for Paris. Al ran to the check-in desk and whatever he said (his Italian was good) he got a seat for the flight. I said I was with him and also needed a seat. Al acted neutral so we both got on the plane and arrived in Paris a couple hours later.

Somehow, I wasn't afraid that he might pull out a knife. So instead of leaving him to find a flight to New York, I decided I should stay with him until we both got back home and I could hopefully find out what the knife incident was all about. I would then decide what to do about our relationship.

We checked into the hotel in Paris. The more conversation we had the more I realized that something about him had gone really wrong. He was not making any sense. He seemed confused and paranoid. I managed to stay the night with him though I did not sleep.

The next morning, his paranoid chatter increased and when we went to a local bakery I asked if I could make a call to the U.S. Embassy. I explained that I was with someone who appeared to be having a breakdown and asked for help.

"The U.S. Embassy is not here to take care of you."

That was it. Then the voice hung up.

We had originally planned to stay one more night

but I wanted to get home as quickly as possible so we had our bags brought down at the hotel and Al followed me into the taxi.

I realized that I did not have to talk to him. All I had to do was take action and he would follow. At the airport I managed to get our tickets honored for the next flight and I kept telling myself that even though I was exhausted I had to get him back on U.S. soil.

When we were served a meal he would not eat but he wrote me a note saying that the food was poisoned. I shared that—and my other concerns—with the stewardesses and they were very nice to me, which made the trip a little more bearable.

Back in New York, we taxied to his apartment after leaving my luggage with my doorman at my building on 59th and First Avenue. I helped Al get settled and then said I was going home. He followed me to the elevator and down into the street and when I started walking south on York Avenue from his building on 81st Street, I noticed that he was walking about ten paces behind me.

Then I noticed him stripping off his clothes one item at a time and throwing them on the street. That's when I knew for sure that something was horribly wrong with him. I kept moving. He kept stripping. As people walked by, I yelled to them to please call the police. When I came to 67th Street, I turned left, hoping to safely reach the inside of New York Presbyterian Hospital.

Al was still following me. As I entered, I saw a security guard.

"See the man walking behind me?" I said to him, still moving. "Please grab him and hold on to him; something is very wrong."

The guard grabbed Al and summoned for help. Al was totally naked by then and was taken to a room. After completing paperwork in the admissions office, he was sent to the psychiatric wing where days later I was told he had suffered a breakdown. I was also told that he was strong and that he would get better. I visited him once but he was on so much medication that he hardly knew who I was.

While I was pleased that I had gotten him back to the U.S., I did not feel that I could marry him. I credit my brother-in-law with making me see that it would have been an unhealthy move.

I never learned what prompted the breakdown but I decided that not responding favorably to getting married in Taormina could not have been the sole catalyst. There must have been other things going on well before we even met. I did know that he had strained relations with his family. Maybe the hectic nature of our trip did not help him, either.

About a month later, after he had been discharged from the hospital, I told Al that I was walking away from our relationship. He kept calling, pleading with me that he had "changed," but he finally stopped after I wrote him a note, asking him not to contact me again.

I never returned to Taormina. However, that experience did not diminish my love of traveling.

But that's another story...

*Family*

## My Immigrant Grandparents

WHILE MY GRANDPARENTS were living, I never asked them why they came to America from Minsk, Russia, and a town in Poland, whose name I never knew. But about 15 years ago, I decided to track their movements by using the Ellis Island database given to them by the Mormon Church. They have done an excellent job of keeping track of ancestors, which I learned is due to a tenet of their religion. And one doesn't have to be Mormon to access this information.

After many tries at name spellings, I found both sets of grandparents. It was no small matter to retrieve the information because immigrants spoke in their accents and the note takers on the island spelled names phonetically, not how they were spelled in their native countries.

The surnames I had to deal with were Katashuk from my Russian Orthodox maternal grandparents, and Stampor from my Roman Catholic paternal grandparents' Polish roots.

Both couples had traveled to Hamburg, Germany,

several years apart during the early 1900's, where they boarded a ship headed for the United States. I found the ship's names and the ledger that reflected the crossings.

In the case of my Russian grandparents, my grandfather sailed first and his wife-to-be followed later. However, "later" turned out to take too long, so without any word between the two, my grandfather sailed back to Europe while my grandmother was on a ship sailing here. When she couldn't find him, she returned to Russia. Apparently, this happened several times before they finally met up, got married and settled in Avoca, Pennsylvania.

My paternal grandparents arrived in America together and settled in Webster, Massachusetts, where, even now, Polish is widely spoken.

Unfortunately, neither set of grandparents ever learned English and my parents refused to teach my sister and I Russian or Polish based on the belief that it was somewhat tacky to speak either of those languages. To this day, I regret not being able to speak either, even though I did study Russian in college and I can read the Cyrillic alphabet.

I also regret never having spoken to any of my grandparents during their life in this country. My maternal grandmother must have been a feisty woman to travel back and forth several times without speaking any local language. My paternal grandparents appear to have been more settled from coming over together and moving straight to Webster. One thing I was told growing up was that my paternal grandmother did not like her new country and regretted the move throughout her life.

I learned from my mother that because she was raised Russian Orthodox my father's parents did not speak to her for years, relenting only when they decided that she made a good wife and mother. It probably helped that my sister and I were raised Catholic, though this was by accident and simply due to the parochial school we attended.

A few years ago, when Ellis Island offered to put up memorial walls displaying the names of those who had passed through the island, I felt that I should at least acknowledge them this way. Every time I visit, I have taken great pleasure seeing their names etched in stone on those walls.

## Oil and Water

My mother was one of four surviving children whose parents came to America from the old Soviet Union and settled in Pennsylvania. When she graduated high school, she announced that she wanted to go to nursing school in Los Angeles, a long way away from her hometown. She graduated three years later and resettled back in New York City, where she met up and married the man who became my father. They had previously met in Rhode Island, where she and her mother had been living with her stepfather.

My father first saw her there and was immediately smitten. She was very beautiful. He got her address and wrote to her often. My mother did not feel comfortable writing back so she asked her sister Alice to answer my father's letters. He never knew about this. When my father finally proposed, my mother's mother told her to marry him because, as she said, "he would be a good provider." So she did and he was.

He bought her gown from B. Altman's and everything else. She wanted lilies to carry and the florist delivered calla lilies, which she did not like, but she used them anyway. They were married in Avoca, Pennsylvania, in her childhood home. The wedding was Russian Orthodox, which my father's parents, who were Catholic, apparently did not appreciate. In fact, they did not extend any kindness toward my mother until after they saw that she was a good and decent person. Then they accepted her.

Once my parents married, my father took care of everything, from purchasing a house to paying the bills and investing some money. This meant that my mother had little to do running the house so when my father died when she was 38 she needed to learn how to do all sorts of things on her own. She started taking college courses at NYU in accounting and investments and became very good at taking over our house, contracting workers when necessary and paying all of the bills. As a result, she became fiercely independent, which was a huge difference from when my father ran the household.

My relationship with my mother was for the most part oil and water. I invariably wore the wrong dress, used an unattractive lip color, cut my hair too short or was too sensitive for her taste.

I left home after becoming a lawyer, and except for the last year of her life, our relationship continued via telephone. Each time we ended our conversation I sat in psychic pain until it slowly dissipated. When I once told her I was truly unhappy at one of my corporate positions and was thinking of leaving, she said that I was "lucky" to have such a job and that I should keep it, which I did for another 10 years and then I quit.

I am convinced that when children become adults, negative memories and impressions of their parents undergo a process of rethinking, which sometimes leads to a new appreciation for things that may have originally seemed less than optimal. This transition can last even well into middle age.

When I reached that point, I stopped focusing on the negatives and remembered that my mother had introduced me to the piano, classical music, opera, ballet and theatre. When I was 14, she told me she thought I could become a lawyer and when I decided to go to law school, she was thrilled. She waited on me hand and foot during those years, leaving me free to study.

Then my mother supported a trait I inherited from my father—traveling! I have now been to all seven continents, visiting over 100 countries—some more than once. She accompanied me sometimes, too.

Her favorite pastime when not traveling or babysitting my sister's children was reading. She read *The Wall Street Journal* and *Barron's* faithfully and preferred biographies over fiction.

By the time she turned 78, her atherosclerosis and dementia had worsened and my sister was having trouble handling her along with her own demanding life of work and children. I told her we should move our mother from Chicago (where my sister and family lived at that point) to me, as I had just moved into a two-bedroom apartment. She arrived with her cat, and for one year we were inseparable once my workday ended. She was too frail to walk so I wheeled her around our neighborhood, cooked for us, rushed her to the hospital when she fell and all the other things that a caregiver does for someone who is challenged in both mind and body.

I felt that it was the least I could do for a mother who had put her children above all else. To her, remarrying was out of the question, as she never wanted to take the chance that we wouldn't have a good stepfather.

When she died, her cat became mine and lived ten more years before passing at the age of 21.

I am very grateful that I woke up one day in my 50's, appreciating what my mother had done, not only with her own life but for mine, as well.

## Leena and Neena

I have been fortunate to fill my apartment with several comfortable pieces of furniture and knickknacks from my many travels over the years. But nothing compares with the two biggest objects of my affection: Leena and Neena—my two cats, who continue giving me pleasure as we move into our third year of living together.

These huge black and white tabby cats are sisters and have never been apart since they were born eight years ago. I can tell them apart because their coloring is somewhat different and their individual facial expressions are also distinctive, though when I first brought them home, I really had to work at defining the differences.

In fact, I almost didn't get Leena and Neena. When my mother's cat, which became mine after she passed away, departed for cat heaven five years ago, I could not see myself replacing her.

Then one day in 2005, I received an email from the North Shore Animal League in Port Washington, Long Island, which I had occasionally supported. They house hundreds of animals for adoption. From time to time, I would get an email about a dog or a cat that was available or a request for a donation. But the email that perked my interest said, "medically challenged cats need a home." Attached, was a short video of the cats, saying that they had been at the League for two years without being re-adopted.

The cats had originally been adopted at birth. Four years later, the family was moving and they could not take the cats so they returned them to the League. Both had heart conditions, and the email also said that the two cats had to be adopted together since they had never been apart and that any new home had to be a quiet place with no other animals or children.

It was no wonder that they were still at the League. But then I realized that my lifestyle fit all the conditions, and the fact that I also have heart issues made my decision a bit easier.

I called the League and made an appointment to meet the cats. Their caregiver, a lovely lady named Dorit, told me I should meet the cats before deciding anything. I asked my friend Bill to drive me to Port Washington. I was taken to their quarters, where they were housed with about 25 other cats. It was so crowded and I wondered how so many cats in one room could be comfortable.

The two sisters were pointed out to me and I observed two scruffy, overweight cats that were very scared and not terribly friendly.

"Do you really want them?" Dorit said.

"Yes," I told her, as I already committed myself to taking them.

"Okay, then let's go through the adoption process while the staff gets them ready," she said, sounding a bit surprised.

The adoption process was amazingly long—three hours long, in fact. Bill became pretty frustrated, as he hadn't planned for this to be an all-day affair.

"If we had seen two cats in the street," he said, "we would have picked them up and that would be that. Here, you have to do paperwork as if you are adopting children."

He was right. There were a lot of official adoption papers to fill out and contracts to sign. Finally, the staff put the cats in carriers and gave them to us. Dorit was so pleased to see them adopted that she gave me cases of food and a variety of cat toys.

We said goodbye to the waving staff and drove home to my apartment. I took the cats out of the carriers and locked them in a room for safety while I literally ran to the nearest pet store to get a bag of litter.

Twenty minutes later, I opened the door to the room and couldn't find them. I looked and looked. Nothing.

*Maybe they escaped through an opening I didn't know about?*

*How am I going to tell the League that I lost them on their first day home?*

I stared into space for a while, shaking my head and wondering what my next step should be. As nightfall came, I tried to rest.

At three in the morning, I got out of bed and went to the room, thinking that the desk in there might have a space under it where the cats could go. I crawled to where I could see under the desk and—voila!—I saw tails.

*Obviously, these cats are very afraid of this totally new experience.*

I decided to let them work their own way out of whatever fear they were feeling. That meant letting them hide under the desk when they needed to, so I did what I could to make it comfortable for them there.

After a few weeks, they let me start to groom them and now their coats have become glossy and smooth. They are still overweight, though I am trying to find ways for them to lose a little without starving them.

Their names at the League were Kruk and Dalton, which seemed strange for female cats. I renamed them Leena and Neena even though they are not responsive to their new names.

Neena, the heaviest one at 16 pounds, insists on sitting on my lap whenever I relax on my living room couch. Leena prefers being petted and groomed in the morning and hangs around me when she is ready to go to her favorite place in the apartment for that activity. All other times when we are together, they get themselves into some really funny positions that always keep me laughing. It's clear that they care for each other, even grooming each other, which I enjoy watching them do.

Over the years, I have taken them back to the North Shore Animal League every six months or so for echocardiograms. I can get these done in the city but then the tests will cost around $500 each. With the League, once one adopts a medically ill animal from them, all their medical issues are treated for free. You just have to get out there!

Neena and Leena lived with me for six years until both died of heart attacks within months of each other. Two months later, feeling that my home was too empty, I adopted two cats named Harley and Gizmo.

## My Father ... A Mixed Legacy

My father worked at home drawing catalogues by hand for Lane Bryant, a clothing store, which still exists today. He painstakingly drew every page, full of models wearing outfits along with descriptive write-ups and prices. I still have some of those catalogues.

He was an artist who had traveled the world before he married my mother. He studied art in Paris and took cruise ships everywhere. He painted still lifes when he had time, but no matter what, our house had to remain on the quiet side whenever he was working. This meant that my sister and I could not romp loudly around the house—ever. He would yell at us if we did, and I recall one time feeling so frustrated at having to stay quiet that I deliberately started yelling in an adjacent room where I knew he would hear me.

I never forgot that incident because it was the one time he said nothing. No yelling. Nothing! I eventually stopped and proceeded to feel guilty about what I had just done. Of course it was only as an adult that I came to appreciate why he needed peace and quiet.

My father kept a cat o' nine tails on his office door, which frightened my sister and me. He used it on me one day (I don't recall why) so whenever he would look at it we would become very quiet. In fact, we were always a little nervous around him because his presence could never be separated from images of that strap.

This is despite the fact that on Sundays he would take some time off to sit with us and play music on the record player. He loved Gilbert and Sullivan, especially *The Mikado*, so that is what we would listen to, and my sister and I eventually came to know every song. To this day, I still know most of the words.

I also remember the year I began to recognize his handwriting on the Christmas gifts we received.

"From Santa."

I was more excited about figuring that out than I was about losing my belief in Santa Claus.

When I was just shy of 14, my father died suddenly

from a heart attack. He was 40. It was a Tuesday in January, and I had just arrived home from my high school where I had started spring semester. It was cold, but our neighbors were gathered outside their houses, which looked strange as I walked down the block to our house. I greeted them all with a smile but they knew something I didn't. As I approached the front door, my aunt greeted me and told me the news. When I was able to process it, I remember feeling somewhat relieved because I would not have to live in fear of that strap anymore. On the other hand, I became shy, and for many years the smile I had always enjoyed was wiped off my face.

My father had been ill with heart problems but my sister and I barely knew anything about it. Our mother never said much about it and I only remember one time when we were blueberry picking, he had to sit down on a rock but we were never told why. There were vials and syringes in the refrigerator, and when I asked my mother about them she just said they were for my father. I never questioned it any further.

We had a buzzer system in the house for him to use if he felt pain, but all I ever found out was that he had an angina attack in the basement and by time my mother came down from the third floor he had died.

They had been married for 17 years.

My mother did not know what to do about the funeral arrangements so she sent his body back to Webster, Massachusetts, where his parents and siblings lived and we went there for the funeral. He was the first one to be buried in a family plot there. My mother took us to visit a few times when we were growing up, but none of us continued going in later years.

I did not have the benefit of a loving relationship with

my father. This had a significant effect on my ability to create a life with a "good" man. That is not to say I didn't have relationships. I did—lots of them, but they were short-lived except for one, and most of them were difficult. *Maybe I wasn't meant to have a soul mate.*

To this day, I have no idea what was in those vials. They remained in our refrigerator for a long time after his death before one day they were suddenly gone.

## Childhood World

I was born October 11, 1937, at around 5:30 p.m. EST in a bedroom of our home in Woodside, Queens. My mother, who was a nurse, felt that hospitals were not clean enough, so she chose to have the doctor deliver me at home.

I was the first born in the family, aside from a collie named Maka that was already in our house. My parents had moved from an apartment on East Ninth Street in Manhattan to a house in Queens because of the dog. Maka and I got along well until one day she was suddenly gone. Although I was quite sad, nothing was explained and I only found out later that he had bitten the postman twice so my father had to give him away. But being exposed to an animal so early in life gave me a loving comfort level around dogs and later cats, which has continued throughout my life.

The house I grew up in at 50-43 64th Street was part of a three-block development of attached houses, each with two stories, a basement and about seven rooms. We had a corner house with a little more land, allowing space for a sandbox for my sister and me. Loretta was born in our house two and a half years later on February 14, 1940, in the middle of a huge snowstorm.

The rooms in our house were rather large, especially compared to most city apartments. The living room was especially big. That's where our family portraits were kept hanging. When I was quite young, my father arranged to have these paintings done by an artist who owed my father some money. Instead of paying him back, my father suggested that the man use his skills to capture our family on canvas. So our whole family, including two of my aunts, sat on a piano stool one at a time and were told to keep very still. We were a normal middle-class family so having portraits hanging in our home was a real treat, like royalty.

The kitchen was also quite spacious with room for a table where most meals were eaten. The dining room was used only on holidays. As young children, we looked forward each evening to our father coming down from his upstairs office to have dinner with us.

One of my favorite family memories took place in our kitchen on the special occasions when my father brought home live lobsters. He would first place a huge pot of water on the stove and while the water was heating he would put the lobsters on the kitchen floor. In those days, the fishmongers did not tie the lobster's claws as they do today. My father would take a wooden spoon or fork and place them on the floor. The lobsters would pick up the utensils and walk around with them. My sister and I would stand outside the kitchen door and watch these very scary creatures crawl around the floor, expecting them to attack us any second.

My father laughed at this before picking up the lobsters and putting them in the boiling water. When I realized we were eating the same lobsters that we had just been watching that were very much alive just minutes earlier, I felt so sorry that these animals had been killed for our dinner! Luckily, our lobster fest was not a common occurrence.

I can also remember—or should I say I can't ever forget—one particularly strange item kept in our refrigerator. One day when I was about 10, my mother asked me why I was staring at some little feet in some kind of gelatin. She explained that it was a dish called "pigs feet," which was my father's favorite meal. I shuddered at the thought of eating any type of animal feet. To this day, I have never eaten such a dish and have never seen it on a restaurant menu. Maybe it can be found only in Poland where my father's parents were from.

My mother was not a particularly good or inventive cook but she did have a tasty menu of dishes that she made for every holiday celebration. Her ham or turkey was always done just right and she was even good at making gravy. Her sweet potatoes with marshmallows were delicious, her corn fritters were to die for and her apple pie was outstanding. I have never found a bakery to compete with hers.

Although I helped her in the kitchen, by the time I hit my teens I was more interested in creating a beautiful dining room table. I have no idea what prompted that, but I do know that I did research on setting tables, flower arrangements and candles, and I enjoyed the total experience of great food served on a great-looking table.

Most of our neighbors were also first-generation, lower- to middle-class Americans, who came mainly from Italy and Ireland. One neighbor was a postal employee while another played the trumpet in Broadway orchestras. Occasionally, he and his wife invited me to go with them to a show. I babysat for them a lot for free and this was a nice way of thanking me. One of their children is a godson of mine.

When I was born, Hitler was in power but the United States had not yet entered the war. I remember saving grease from cooking, which my mother kept in jars, and taking them to our local butcher so it could be made into soap. My father was not at risk of being drafted because of his heart condition and having a family.

I was about nine or ten when my parents bought a Zenith television set. We were almost the first family on the block to have one.

Buster Crabbe became an idol of mine because of his good looks and his acting in the *Flash Gordon* movies, which I loved. I found out how to get his home phone number in New Jersey and tried calling him one day but did not get through. So I wrote to him. When he mentioned my name on his show, citing me as a fan, I was thrilled. My parents were not pleased with the fact that I called New Jersey from New York because that was expensive in those days, but I was ecstatic that Buster Crabbe mentioned my name.

My mother and I loved the courtroom drama *Perry Mason,* which we started watching in about 1957. My mother particularly liked his assistant, Stella. Since she was not a lawyer, I found it curious that my mother would later say that she thought I should become a lawyer. Was it that women did not become lawyers or did she quietly feel that I would not make a good lawyer? We never discussed it.

When not in school or doing homework or watching television, the kids in the neighborhood gathered together to play street games, such as hopscotch, jacks and stickball. We would play until we heard the sound of the ice cream truck approaching. I still remember what a treat it was getting a cone from the ice cream man.

When it was time to move up from middle school, the nuns encouraged us all to attend a Catholic high school on Long Island, which would require a train ride back and forth every day. Since I was still having a lot of colds, my mother decided I should go to the local public high school of 4,000 students because it was much closer. It was a difficult four years because I simply did not fit in. Whatever hip was in those days, I was not it.

I graduated from high school having to take the history regents twice. I hated history because it was so poorly taught in those days and I could not simply memorize a bunch of facts about wars.

I was a difficult child for my mother. I cried a lot, slept a lot and argued a lot. I was extremely sensitive and I remember my mother's expression of frustration in simply not knowing what to say or do for me.

*Did my moods have anything to do with my father's sudden death when I was a teenager? I do not know!*

Years later, during one of our travels together, something prompted me one evening to ask my mother if she loved me. I told her that I had no idea if she did or not, because she never said anything to cause me to believe that she did.

"Everyone's mother loves her children," she said.

It was a very indirect way of saying she loved me, which I found difficult to appreciate at the time. But as the years went by, I was able to realize that she did care about me even if she did not understand my needs. And I will never forget her ecstatic reaction when I passed the bar on my first attempt!

## Loretta

*Ambivalence can be painful. My sister, Loretta, has stage IV gastric cancer, diagnosed barely a year ago. She is 68. She initially agreed to have chemo treatments, but after eight rounds she was completely wiped out and refused to have any more. The doctors cannot offer any prognosis for how long she has, as they have few statistics on this very rare form of cancer. The protocol is to keep her on medication to control the pain, infusions to keep her hydrated and with food she can eat without throwing up—all to insure that her days are comfortable until some other condition may arise.*

*Ten days ago, recognizing her general state of confusion, the home visiting nurse recommended that Loretta undergo hospice care for a while so that they could study her and pinpoint why she is struggling.*

*They found an infection, which they are treating with an antibiotic, but while the infection may be the sole cause of her confusion, it is unlikely, considering her cancer.*

*Last Friday, I received a call advising me that the doctors have agreed that she has only days or weeks left. I spent Saturday and part of Sunday at the hospice in Philadelphia, together with other family members. I had to return home but I hope that Sunday was not the last time I will see her.*

*Loretta has lost so much weight. She is simply skin and bones. There is nothing left in her body able to fight the cancer. She is still confused. They inserted a tube so she does not have to get out of bed to pass water.*

*How can we wish for her to recover and at the same time wish for closure so that we don't have to watch her suffer any longer?*

> *We are all lucky that none of us have unresolved issues with Loretta, which would make her passing all the more difficult. Nevertheless, the ambivalence is painful as each hour passes. I am guessing that if she dies without having processed what is happening to her, which up to now she has not, I would feel relieved that she is no longer suffering. But for now, the ambivalence remains.*

I wrote this just before Loretta passed away on Monday, June 1, 2009, at about 9:30 in the morning. Alice Ann, her youngest daughter, and Alice Ann's mother-in-law, Gay LoCascio, had just walked into Loretta's room to hear her last breath. While I was saddened when I received the phone call, I felt relieved as well that Loretta was no longer suffering. Carol Sue, Loretta's eldest daughter, organized a beautiful church ceremony and luncheon. Many family and friends attended the service. Carol Sue gave a beautiful eulogy. Loretta was cremated and her urn is buried in a cemetery near Pittsburgh—next to her first child, who died in a freak accident at the age of 15 months, another tragedy.

On a snowy Valentine's Day when I was two-and-a-half years old, my life completely changed when Loretta was born. That event compounded the shock of losing my dog and best friend, Maka, who had been returned to the pound after biting the postman one too many times. Without Maka, I was left alone to watch this new baby get lots of attention. She was a bubbly blonde with blue-green eyes and always laughing.

I felt dumped during those early years. Was it because I had dark eyes and dark hair? Or was it that I did not laugh a lot like she did? Years later, my mother told me that I was too serious and that this bothered my parents. My mother had no idea that I felt I had been dumped.

As Loretta and I grew, it became clear that our differences were much deeper than our looks. We had very different personalities. While I was studious in school, Loretta thought that the only purpose of going to school was to make friends. I usually did homework in the house but Loretta was always inviting neighborhood friends over for fun and games. I would yell at her to be quiet. She would laugh at me.

As children, Loretta and I did not know why our father worked at home. He just did and we accepted it. However, our mother decided that the house was too crowded because of that arrangement so she decided to go back to work as a nurse. She was never around during the day, as she was either working a day shift or home asleep after a night shift. On most days, I took it upon myself to clean the kitchen after breakfast and would tell Loretta to do her share. But she would just laugh and never washed a single dish. I used to write notes to our mother, telling her that Loretta was not doing any work. My mother never answered my notes. I found out much later that she simply thought the notes were cute and didn't require an answer!

When our father died, it came as a total shock to Loretta and I because we had no idea of the seriousness of his illness. I recall hearing our mother saying from time to time that "he did not feel well," but Loretta and I never thought that it was anything life threatening. We were both in denial for several years before we realized what happened.

When it became Loretta's turn to attend high school, she picked a different school than me, which put some distance between us. After school, I was in my room doing homework while Loretta would come home just in time for dinner after spending the afternoon in a coffee shop with her friends.

When I came home after two years away at college in Virginia and transferred to Columbia University, Loretta was leaving to attend college in Pittsburgh. Our separation was becoming more and more physical after years of living separate emotional lives.

Loretta met her husband at college and they married just after she graduated.
They moved to Michigan. I went off to England and we grew further apart.

Over the next 40 years, another change slowly took place, as Loretta became closer to the person I was and I became more like who she used to be. As I began to laugh more and more, Loretta became the serious one. She was concerned with raising her children and opening a business with her husband, which was very stressful even though it has been successful.

Aside from the issue of serious versus fun loving, we came to have very little in common except our core values. In all other ways, we were opposites.

I was actually surprised when Loretta asked me to be godmother to her first child. When more children came along, she never hesitated to let me take them on trips, even far away, when I asked. I have spent most holiday celebrations with her and her family and cherish my great relationship with her adult children and their children.

When I learned she had been diagnosed with cancer and had decided to come from Philadelphia to Sloan Kettering in New York for treatment, I attended every doctor's meeting and sat with her through many of her chemo treatments.

I wouldn't have done it any other way, yet when I think about our childhood I am astounded that I didn't hate her. Perhaps it was my coming to the realization that family is incredibly important and family members do not have to be your soul mates in order to be loved. They are loved simply because they are family.

As sisters, Loretta and I had no similarities in looks or personality, but our core values were aligned with how we viewed the world and the people in it. Because of our differences we were not close friends. We did not talk every day or even every week.

While these separations allowed each of us to be who we were, I knew all along that other siblings go their own ways and still stay close with everyday phone calls, etc.

I remain puzzled about why our relationship was good but not close. We never shared secrets or confided in each other, except on rare occasions. It was almost as if we were neighbors, not sisters. Nevertheless, in all our years we respected the fact that we each had a sister and that simply meant that no matter what, we would support one another.

After Loretta died, I spent months in a support group at Gilda's Club, airing my own sorrow. When they asked me what brought me there, I said, "to stop crying."

Loretta and Peter had enjoyed a whirlwind romance at Duquesne University. Two years older, Pete was popular on campus and after dating through college he proposed to her when she was a senior by coming to Queens and asking my mother for her approval to give Loretta an engagement ring. My mother said yes and we spent the rest of the summer looking for a place for the wedding. They went to Jamaica on their honeymoon.

Life seemed perfect for them. Loretta got pregnant

almost immediately and they had a son, J. John, named after our father. They were living in Ann Arbor, Michigan, where Pete had been accepted for a doctorate program in pharmaceutical sciences.

One day, Pete announced that he was going to the lab to retrieve a book and Loretta asked him to take J. John. Pete said he did not want to because it was going to be a quick trip. Loretta insisted and Pete gave in. He put J. John in the car seat and took him along when he went in to the lab. Pete lost sight of J. John for a mere two seconds and in that time J. John put a vile in his mouth. Pete rushed him to the hospital with the vile but since no one knew what was in it, J. John died after convulsing for a couple of hours.

Loretta was determined to move on with their lives, so conversations with Pete about J. John rarely, if ever, took place. Pete had to bury his emotions. Although they agreed to counseling, they were only told to get pregnant again, which they did to the tune of three more children. Loretta never told her three other children about J. John. I stepped in just a few years ago and told them. To say they were in shock would be an understatement, but they have come to accept not being told as they recognize the pain the death must have been.

After receiving his doctorate, Pete's first position was with Smith Kline in Philadelphia. They bought a house in an estate sale, which needed fixing up and Loretta spent a few years redesigning it. That's when Pete announced that he accepted a position at American Home, which meant they had to move to Westchester. That home needed fixing, too, and by the time Loretta got that done, Pete declared that he wanted to quit his job and take another position in Chicago. So Loretta moved the family again.

A couple of years later, Pete announced that he wanted to start a business of his own in New Jersey and that he needed Loretta's help. So Loretta moved to Philadelphia and began looking for physical space across the bridge in New Jersey for their pharmaceutical-related business.

The business opened with both Pete and Loretta as officers and within a year they were doing very well. Then Pete announced that it was important to open a satellite office in Europe. Loretta moved to Windsor, England, while Pete stayed behind to run the New Jersey office. After two years, Pete got an offer for the company that he felt he could not refuse. Loretta did not agree, but she came back from England and signed the documents, selling their company while staying as consultants. But it didn't take long before Pete and Loretta decided it was not a good fit and they quit when their contract ended.

Then Pete decided to start another new company doing the same thing as before, knowing that it would compete with his former company. Once again, Loretta went out looking for new physical space and they began all over again.

Five years later, they decided to plan their retirement, leaving the company to be run by their eldest daughter.

For years, Loretta had suffered from stomachaches but would not take time to get medical attention. She just popped tons of Tylenol and would say that she was sure it was just nerves. When she finally did go to a doctor, she was diagnosed with a rare kind of stage IV stomach cancer.

Everyone was thrown for a loop. We all bought books, looked up hospitals and doctors, did endless research online and looked for support groups. This event changed everyone who knew and loved Loretta. Pete dropped everything and catered to Loretta's every request. He did this for the one year she had left. When she died, he was in shock. She had been his rock for almost 50 years and he could not accept that she was no longer there for him.

Pete is still depressed, sad and miserable. I know from my own experience that we remain alone in our suffering. Pete is alone in dealing with his loss. No one can replace what she was to him. So I forget about my feelings of anger as I become aware of his loss and try to be sensitive to the fact that he has lost his better half—a fate worse than his own death.

May she rest in peace.

*My parents*

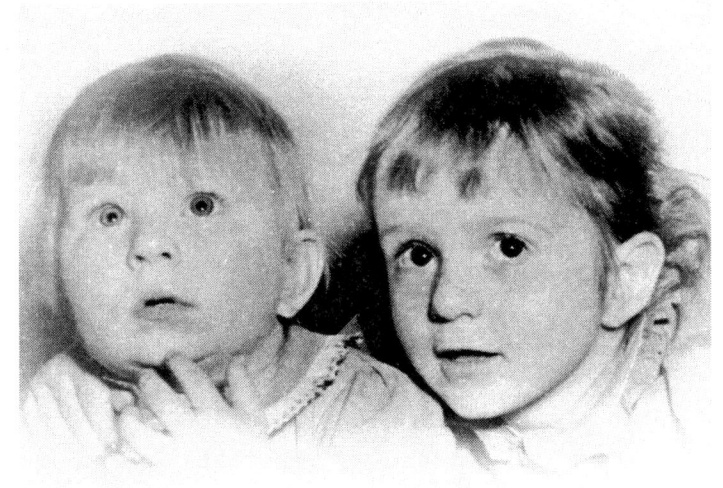

*Above: Loretta and me; below: 50-43 64th Street, Woodside*

*Me, myself and I!*

*My mother*

*Above: Aunt Alice (left) and Sister Ligouria (right);
Below: Loretta and me, with our parents*

*My father and me, 1948*

*Above: Loretta and Pete, 1998; below: Christmas 2000*

*Above: Gwen and me; below: my 75th birthday*

# Sister Ligouria

Aunt Sophia joined a convent in Connecticut at the age of 14 and eventually became Sister Ligouria. She was always kind and accepting, and during my early years she often suggested that I consider joining the convent myself. Thankfully, she stopped doing this when I made it clear that I had no interest.

To me, a convent represented an incredibly strict life. For example, when my father died in 1951, she was not permitted to attend her own brother's funeral. In fact, visiting anyone outside the convent was frowned upon, which I found almost inhuman.

Aunt Sophia once told me how she had been tempted to leave the convent when she was in her late teens and again in her early 20's but reneged because she felt her parents would be too sad. For most Polish Catholic families at that time, having a child become a nun or a priest was highly regarded.

Over the years, I noticed that the church sometimes lifted its strict rules on dress (such as the habit), visitation rights and travel policy. At one point, Aunt Sophia received permission to visit Italy to see the motherhouse of her order, and then on to Poland to visit her parents' birthplace. Since her Order would not pay for the trips, I did, as I was glad to give her the opportunity to have those memorable experiences.

As Aunt Sophia aged, I was grateful to know that the convent would take care of her right up until the end, which they did. The only thing she ever complained about was the food.

"Rubber chicken," she often said. "The only good food they make is Polish."

Since her order was Polish, many sisters knew how to cook the Polish way. My aunt spoke fluent Polish and enjoyed being in that atmosphere.

Several years ago, with permission granted from the convent, I drove to Connecticut and picked her up to take a trip to Massachusetts for a family wedding. When we got hungry en route, I pulled off the highway into a McDonald's, the only place I could find, and immediately wondered what I would eat as I had never been inside a fast food chain. Aunt Sophia wanted a hamburger and after staring at the menu I finally found a salad I could order.

For my aunt, the hamburger was like filet mignon. She was in heaven! And much to my surprise, I found the salad quite delicious.

"Oh my," I said. "I just found something healthy to eat in a McDonald's."

During her convent life, she acquired a master's degree in music. She had learned to play piano and organ and eventually became the organist in the convent and at the parish church for Sunday Mass and other occasions. She loved teaching children at the parish school and they loved her, too. For several years, she served as the school's principal. When she retired, she began offering private piano lessons for children, which she continued well into her late 80's.

Sister Ligouria passed quietly one night in 2012, well into her 90's. I remember my aunt fondly as a very kind and loving person.

May she also rest in peace.

## Becoming Aunt Alice

*"Twinkle, twinkle little star..."*

My Aunt Alice taught me that song.

My mother had three siblings. The only one I had any relationship with was her older sister, my Aunt Alice, who lived near us, which was probably why we saw her a lot.

She would read to me whenever she visited and she also taught me to sing. When I was about 10 years old, she married again and subsequently had a son, my cousin Dan. They often visited our home, especially after my father died, when they came to Sunday dinners and all holiday celebrations.

As I grew older, I always stayed close to Aunt Alice.

While I was living at home during law school she asked me if I would teach Dan to play the piano. I had been taking piano lessons since I was six and had kept up my studies for many years. I agreed on the condition that he practiced between lessons. He was a good student and I enjoyed the experience over several years. In fact, one summer I taught piano at a music school on Long Island.

While living in London and then Michigan, I saw little of Aunt Alice. When I returned to New York City to live and work, I saw more of her and her family, mainly on holidays since I was very busy with my career.

One year, I decided to take a trip to Eastern Europe and my mother asked if I would take Aunt Alice. I suspected that it might not be the most comfortable thing for me to do, but I agreed. She was so happy to be invited and to know that we would be visiting the parts of Russia where my maternal family came from.

The trip itself was wonderful, but I found being with her every day kind of difficult. Aunt Alice had never traveled anywhere before and since I had already been to many places on my own, this became challenging.

As the years passed, I realized that of all the relatives I had my aunt was the one who had given me the most attention when I was young. I realized that no matter what, I must make an effort to keep up with her. So every few months, I rented a car and drove north about two-and-a-half hours from New York City, where she lived at the time, to stay for the weekend.

Whenever I would offer to treat her and her husband to a dinner out, my aunt would refuse.

"I don't like going to restaurants," she said, "because I don't trust what they put in the food."

I accepted her response even though I usually ate out back home in the city. But I must admit, I am becoming a bit more like her on this issue. Aunt Alice cooked every meal and they were always simple and healthy. There was a time when I did not pay much attention to what that meant, but I certainly do now.

Aunt Alice kept herself mentally busy by reading and taking up Spanish, which she did by getting books and teaching it to herself. I suppose she inspired me to start taking French classes. She was always impressed that I had studied Russian way back in college and could still read the Cyrillic letters.

I have come to realize that Aunt Alice really did make a difference in my life. Although it is said that daughters grow up and become like their mothers, in this case, I am becoming my Aunt.

## Gizmo and Harley

If Harley had her way, I would never leave my apartment. I would never get up from my living room sofa and she would never get off my lap. Gizmo would never leave my side, either. That's for sure.

I think that's what they call bonding. On the other hand, it could be they miss their previous life so much they are clinging to what they have now. In any case, I can't consider ever parting with them until I have to.

Although I have cherished every cat I ever adopted, Gizmo and Harley, now 16 and 18, are among my favorites. I inherited their names when I blindly agreed to take them in June 2012 from a family that was moving to a building that did not allow pets.

Harley and Gizmo have distinct personalities. Harley is a very active cat with snow-white fur and green eyes. She utters a soft sound when she wants wet food. She uses the same sound when she feels that I have slept enough and wants me to let her rest beside me in bed. This usually occurs around five in the morning. Sometimes I let her in, and when I do, Gizmo, a calico cat of three colors, invariably joins us.

Harley had digestive problems when I first got her. My vet suggested I use a different product and what a difference! Harley no longer throws up every day like she used to early on in our relationship.

Gizmo recently exhibited what I consider strange behavior, especially for her. She was making sounds and letting me pet her for long periods. This was not typical Gizmo, so I took her to my vet, who diagnosed a hyperthyroid condition. The vet also noticed some weight loss, a typical symptom of this problem. The vet explained a treatment that could cure Gizmo but the doctor who specializes in these treatments said that Gizmo's blood level was not high enough to do the procedure. So I continue monitoring Gizmo's weight and if there is any more unusual loss I will return to the vet and go from there. I will do whatever it takes to cure Gizmo because I want to see her laid-back personality come back.

Harley does not like it when I give Gizmo any special attention but since Harley gets so much of it herself I do nothing about her negative attitude. I have noticed that Gizmo will give Harley a whack if Harley passes her. Still, they clearly tolerate one another and me.

## My Ballet Debut

St. Mary's Help of Christians on 69th Street was a 15-minute walk from our home on 61st Street in Queens. The teachers were Irish Catholic nuns. On Saturdays during the school year, I took ballet lessons in a dance studio in Sunnyside. There was also a dance studio near the school on 69th Street that most of my fellow students attended.

During our last year in grammar school, the nuns announced that we would all have an opportunity to try out for a show that had ballet numbers. I was so excited! The director of the 69th Street dance studio put together the choreography and promised to teach it to her students who attended St. Mary's. The nuns were delighted to have this help.

When I applied to be in the show, I was rejected because since I did not take dance lessons in that studio they figured I couldn't possibly be taught the choreography.

I was incredibly disappointed. To make things worse, the girls who were chosen laughed at me because I was not going to be included. The ache persisted.

*What can I do to get the nuns to change their mind and let me be in the show?*

I thought and thought and finally remembered that the nuns had said I could not be in the show because I did not attend the 69th Street dance school like the other girls so they weren't necessarily rejecting me; they were just making it easier for themselves.

I asked my mother if I could switch to the school on 69th Street, even though it meant a longer walk to get there. She agreed, and of course there was a lot of anxiety adjusting to a new place where, except for my classmates, I knew no one. Once I made the change, the nuns said I could be in the show.

Despite the fact that some of the other girls still made fun of me, I ignored them and stuck with the routine of going to that school for the several months we rehearsed the choreography for the show. I was very happy to be in it.

As soon as the show ended, I quietly quit the 69th Street dance school and went back to the studio near our home. The ache disappeared. I continued taking ballet lessons there until I finished high school.

## I Like to Work!

In the summer of 1955, I walked around the city searching for clothing stores where I could ask for a job. My mother frowned on the idea because she felt that we didn't need the money so I should just enjoy the summer. Years later,

I learned that she had been afraid I might enjoy menial work and forego college, which was not the vision she had for her daughters. She had always wanted me to take up law and my sister to go into medicine.

But I was persistent. After being turned down in several stores, I managed to meet with a human resource person at Lane Bryant. I told the gentleman that my father had worked there for at least ten years doing layout and design work. He even created the logo that the store adopted and kept for some 50 years.

I knew that they weren't hiring for the summer but I just kept telling him that I would do anything that was needed. He finally offered me a stock girl position in women's clothing. I was very happy and worked hard, although I kept noticing that the head of the department basically sat around all day. Of course I knew nothing about being the head of a women's clothing department. On the last day of my job, knowing I would not be coming back, I told her that I felt she did nothing all summer. I shudder now when I think of what I said.

That fall, I left for college at Mary Washington College of the University of Virginia in Fredericksburg, Virginia. I initially liked it because the campus was so beautiful. It was essentially a finishing school for girls (no boys), and I felt it would enable me to study harder. I joined the chorus and had fun touring different schools to perform. I also played piano in the school band. However, as a northeastern Catholic (two strikes against me) in a heavily Baptist southern environment, I ultimately felt like an outsider.

I told my mother I would be looking to transfer after my second year. When I got accepted to the General Studies Program at Columbia University, I spent the next two years commuting from Queens to Columbia. I enjoyed the coed atmosphere and joined a choral group, which mostly sang Gregorian chants. I also joined the Catholic group on campus and met some great men and women. Everyone was going off to grad school so I considered the London School of Economics or law school.

After graduating Columbia in 1959 with a degree in Economics, I began my studies at Brooklyn Law School. During the first semester, I began working as a secretary/personal assistant to a professor who was also the president of a historical society. In exchange for working a few hours a week, my tuition was free. I kept the job until I graduated.

When I told my mother about the job, her response was similar to when I first looked for summer work. She asked me again why I worked if I didn't really need to.

"Because I like working," I said.

## The Search Is Over

My first school was P.S. 78 on Maurice Avenue in Woodside. It seemed like I was always catching colds there, which angered my mother who blamed it on the school, so she put me in the local Catholic school taught by nuns, which my sister also attended.

My father was raised as a Roman Catholic and one of his sisters went into a convent at age 14 while another family member became a priest. But he did not pressure us to become Catholic. There was no pressure to adopt any religion from my mother, who was raised as a non-practicing Russian Orthodox.

But there I was, steeped in the Catholic tradition. This

meant Latin masses, the ritual of baptism, confirmation at age 12, the belief that Roman Catholicism was the only religion to follow if one wanted to ascend to heaven, the belief in a limbo and acceptance that Mary was a virgin.

*Did I believe in all this?*

Well, I did not disbelieve, but there was something troubling about the issue of Mary as a virgin. Even though I did not know much about conception, I did know that it took two people to conceive. Nevertheless, I kept the faith. I even sang in the church choir when I lived in London many years later.

One day, when I was back in New York working as an attorney, I walked into Sunday Mass and saw something completely different from the traditional altar, crucifix and other items that normally adorn a Catholic church. I sat in the pew, feeling something odd going on inside me.

When the priest came out to begin the mass, I saw a stage instead of an altar and an actor in costume, not a priest in priestly robes. I cannot explain this, but it frightened me so I walked out of the church that day and never returned.

For years, I wondered why this incident had occurred. I had never experienced any trauma that could have caused this to happen. When my sister's first child died from a bizarre catastrophe a few years before, I had not received any consolation from my religion. Many years later, when I asked a priest about why good people die before their time he had no explanation except to say that we have to keep the faith. I also remember reading a book by a rabbi about why bad things happen to good people, which gave me some modicum of comfort but no real answers.

I don't think it was the death of my nephew that caused me to leave the church. I think it was more that I could no longer believe that Catholicism represented the only true religion. It was simply a business, like any other.

The fact that there are many religions, creeds and philosophies reveals the human desire to want to believe in something that answers their particular questions about life. In my own personal quest, I studied a number of other spiritual concepts. I followed Buddhism for a while after I bought a "Buddha Bible" and read it during a business trip to Tokyo. I thought the teachings were very realistic.

After that period, I joined Theosophy and considered following leaders who claimed that they had reached Nirvana. I have also taken courses at the School of Practical Philosophy in New York City. I have read the works of such writers as Deepak Chopra, the Vietnamese monk Thich Nhat Hanh, Eckhart Tolle and Karen Armstrong, a former nun who has written many books about various religions.

None of this ever convinced me that there is only one right way of thinking about life, except to live it morally and ethically. In fact, no religion has called to me in any meaningful, lasting way. While I believe that there must be a higher power or an initial catalyst of some kind, I have come to absolutely no further conclusions or even guesstimates as to the how and why of the world. Furthermore and thankfully, I feel no need to continue the search.

## Gwen

Gwen was raised in Australia and came to London in the summer of 1963 to get away from a relationship with a married man. I arrived in London that September after spending six weeks traveling around Europe. I planned to spend some time there until my scheduled departure on the Queen Mary back to New York.

I had graduated from law school that year but had encountered difficulty securing a legal position in New York because female attorneys weren't yet being hired there. So I took the first-class ship ticket my mother gave me when I passed the bar exam and made my way across the ocean.

About a week before I was to sail home, I was sitting in my London hotel room one day, musing about what I would face when I returned. I figured I would probably face exactly the same prejudice against female attorneys as I had before. After all, I had only been gone for six weeks.

I recalled an interview at a corporation where I was told that company policy stated that they did not hire women in their law department but that I was being interviewed out of curiosity!

*If that's what I'm going back to, why not stay in London?*

I began looking at newspaper ads for legal positions with a solicitor, as well as ads showing flats for rent or people who were looking for roommates. One ad in particular stood out.

"Quiet Australian lady looking for room in a flat."

I called the number listed and when a woman answered I explained that I might be in a similar position and was calling to find out if she had received any responses. Gwen said she had about 20 replies and would be pleased to share them with me. Then we realized that our hotels were close by so we agreed to meet for lunch the next day.

When we arrived at the restaurant Gwen had chosen, I noticed that she was probably a little older than me (nine years, I later learned), but she was attractive and easy going. We shared stories of why we were in London (Gwen was a consultant in the fashion industry) and she invited me to go with her to see the various flats she already knew about, even though our intention at that point was to look separately.

I wasn't even sure if I could work in London, but in any event, we visited lots of places and found the searching exhausting and the rents staggering, prompting neither of us to settle on an apartment.

When Gwen later told someone how frustrated we were, he said he knew of a one bedroom flat that was available right away, although he wasn't sure when the legal renter would be returning. This didn't sound too stable but we agreed to have a look.

The flat was nicely furnished and it was obviously much better than what we had earlier seen. However, it meant that we had to consider sharing it, as neither one of us could afford the full rent. It didn't take us very long to agree about taking the place even though we were two strangers agreeing to live together in a very nice section of London near Hyde Park.

As soon as we signed a contract, I realized that I urgently needed a job!

I called home to say that I might be staying longer in London. I immediately began to approach legal firms, who told me that while it would be nice to hire me they did not want to go through the hassle of getting me a work permit.

I did note that no one asked if I could type.

By October, Gwen and I were learning about each other and figuring out how to share our living space and organize our meals. On Friday evenings, we treated ourselves at Biagi's, an Italian restaurant next door, a tradition we continued for more than a year. Years later, we returned to this restaurant and were so pleased that the waiters remembered us.

One day in particular sticks out for me from our time in London. When Jack Kennedy was shot, I was in the flat when the phone rang and I heard the news. Gwen had met up with a group of Australians working for a London newspaper. When they heard the news, they called Gwen, as they knew she was sharing a flat with an American. They wanted to give *me* their condolences and came to meet me and offer their thoughts.

I was awed by this reception. Gwen knew more people than I suspected and so many of them wanted to be with an American because of this tragedy. We never again had so many people in the flat at one time.

Gwen and I remained there until the lease ended a year later, when we moved to another place we stayed in until March 1965.

Despite our different upbringing and cultural differences, Gwen and I respected each other and got along pretty well. In fact, we shared more similarities with each other than we did with the English.

I had started dating an Englishman who worked in the government. I knew he would stay in England because of his career and I was not ready to emigrate there. I thought I should come home before I got used to being an Anglophile.

So Gwen was a little upset when I told her it was time for me to return to the U.S. We had enjoyed so much together, especially during the many weekends we spent hopping to other places, like Paris.

As it turned out, Gwen met an accountant in London after I left and they eventually married and had a child a year later. I was asked to be a godmother and Gwen and Pat waited six months until I could take a break from work to go to London for the occasion. Every few years I made a trip to where they had moved in England or they would come together to the States to celebrate Christmas with my family and me.

No matter how long we are apart, it always seems like Gwen and I have never parted whenever we meet again. We simply pick up right where we left off as if there has been no break.

We have always been able to share our happy moments and those that are not—including my boyfriends and her divorce—and always without judgment.

Now, we share the joy of her son Kit, his wife Sonja and their four children. My visits to the U.K. often include a visit, if not a stay, at their home in West Sussex as well as Gwen's flat in Bath.

My most recent week with Gwen at her now assisted-living quarters was great and I hope to return there soon.

Gwen and I have been friends for more than 45 years.

# An Ethical Dilemma

During the eight years I spent in grammar school being taught by Irish nuns, I aimed to keep my grades in the 90's, and most of the time I proudly met my goals. However, just before finishing this period of my education, I ran into trouble during a midterm exam when I became aware of some nervous movement around me. I tried to ignore it but I couldn't help noticing that some students were passing paper around. I decided to mind my own business and complete the exam.

Soon after the midterms were over, one of the nuns asked me to leave the classroom, which I did. One never disobeyed a nun in those days, and being 12 years old, I wasn't about to test that.

I was brought into another room and told to sit in front of several nuns, who asked me if I had taken part in any cheating. I said that I did not cheat or help anyone else to do anything like that.

The nuns appeared to have no difficulty with my response, but then they asked me to name any students that I thought or knew had cheated. I was sure that one boy had been cheating, but I refused to share that information. The nuns were very angry that I wouldn't tattletale, but I thought it was the right thing to do.

Then they told me I could go back to my classroom. I believed at the time that I had not said anything about anyone cheating. But when midterm report cards were handed out, I got a 65 in each test—all D's—a real catastrophe for me.

As soon as I saw those grades, tears starting flowing down my face. All my good work over all those years was rendered meaningless in that moment. I wondered if I should say something, as I knew which students had been cheating, but once again, I chose to say nothing.

I told my mother. She listened, said nothing, and let me stay home the next day. The matter was never mentioned again in class, but when final exams came around I made a point of not sitting anywhere near those students.

When the next report cards were handed out, my grades were back in the 90's. The nuns had not considered those D's as part of the final grade. I was extremely relieved, but the experience stayed with me for years, and I continued to ask myself if I had been ethical by not saying anything. Maybe it would have been better to tell the nuns what I knew. Maybe. I have never been able to answer that question.

## *Scammed?*

I was waiting in the Amtrak station for my train to Philadelphia when a young man, who appeared to be in his 20's, approached me.

"Could you give me 75 cents?" he asked. "I need to buy a ticket that costs 12 dollars, but I'm short 75 cents. I thought I had my credit card, but it turns out I grabbed a non-credit card instead, so I can't charge it."

He showed me a card, which looked like a gift card to some store.

"What train costs twelve dollars?" I said.

"The train to Patchogue," he said. "I'll give you my work number so you can call and confirm that this is the town I am in."

I noticed he did not say home number.

"In fact," he said, "I work at a restaurant and if you came there I will ensure that you eat for free."

I guess I didn't look suitably impressed so he

continued speaking.

"It's a very upscale restaurant," he said.

He took notice of me opening my purse and probably assumed I would be giving him what he needed. In fact, I had decided to scrounge around in my bag and see what kind of change I could find.

I looked again at this young man and noticed a very clean cut rather attractive person with nice blue eyes. I asked myself if this might be a new type of scam, and since I wasn't sure I thought I might give him whatever change I could grab, even if it wasn't the full amount or even if it were more. I was giving him the benefit of the doubt.

"Shall I give you my number or the name of the restaurant?" he said, as I handed

him the change.

"Not necessary," I said. "I usually stick to the city for eating out, but thanks."

The young man thanked me and walked away in the opposite direction of any ticket counter. I wondered if he had just conned me. If so—and I still have doubts—I hope I reached my quota for the year.

But that's another story . . .

*Health*

## Mission Accomplished—Finally!

"THE BOYS WON'T like me!"

That was my biggest concern when my vision began to erode around the age of twelve and I was diagnosed with myopia. That's because I was convinced that boys would never like girls wearing corrective glasses. I felt so unattractive when I had to put them on in class. I don't know how I survived the embarrassment.

I continued wearing glasses throughout high school, college and law school, and with each visit to the eye doctor my glasses got thicker.

While living in London after law school, I heard that Russian scientists were developing a high-tech process that could somehow restore a person's vision back to normal. I thought of going there to find out for myself, but even though I studied Russian in college, my ability to converse in that language was primitive and would simply not be good enough to ask questions and understand the answers. So I didn't go.

When I returned to the States, I happily accepted an

invitation to join the legal department of Dow Chemical Company in Midland, Michigan. I was being hired as an attorney, not just an assistant or secretary. Finally, there was a law on the books—which did not exist when I graduated law school—that prohibited companies from discriminating against women.

Soon after I settled into my life in Midland, I heard about an outstanding local optometrist who was selling a product called "contact lenses" to replace glasses.

*Oh my, could this really be true?*

I made an appointment right away and couldn't wait for the day to come.

"What *are* these things and can I get them?"

I was full of questions.

"Yes you can," the optometrist said, "but I need to tell you that it will take time to get used to because you will be literally placing a cup as it were over each eye."

"I don't care!" I said. "Let's do it."

He measured my eyes and told me he had to send away for lenses that would match my size and strength.

A week or two later, he handed me the lenses, along with a cleaner, a bottle of rinsing fluid and a pouch to keep everything in every night. There was a lot of paraphernalia to go along with the lenses but I didn't care. I was so happy to be getting rid of my glasses.

Putting the lenses in my eyes for the first time was incredibly frightening because it is not normal to touch that part of the body so directly. It was hard to keep my eyes open long enough to get used to the lenses. I know it looked like I was sleeping half the time, but I was grateful that no one at the office laughed at me. At least a month went by before I was able to feel comfortable putting them on and taking them out.

A year later, I decided to return to New York City. Living in such a small town wasn't totally for me, but I never regretted moving there because of the legal training I received on the job. And I will always remember the optometrist who introduced me to contact lenses!

Eventually, options improved and I was able to see a specialist who replaced the large glass ones I had been wearing for a much smaller lens that fit only over the retina. They were considerably lighter and easier to get used to. They worked for about five years and then I learned about soft lenses, including the ones you can wear day and night. Naturally, I switched to this new generation of contacts.

During this time, my doctor told me I had a scar in one eye and that I should have it removed. I did nothing about it until I heard of a brand new technique using a laser beam to restore poor vision back to normal. This is probably what the Russians were working on.

When the procedure gained FDA approval, I went to a doctor in New Jersey to see if I could become one of his first guinea pigs but he turned me down because he was not yet permitted to work on someone whose vision was as bad as mine.

Then I tried the head of eye surgery at Manhattan Eye and Ear. The doctor confirmed that he could do the laser surgery for me but first he would have to shave off the scar that I had.

"Whatever we need to do," I said.

I was nervous when the day came for the scar surgery. They had to give me valium to calm me down. The surgery went much better than I expected, but I had to wait months before the doctor felt comfortable about operating on that eye. Eventually, I had laser surgery on both of my eyes. I did not have to wear glasses of any kind for years until I recently began needing reading glasses.

For nearly 40 years, I dealt with the positive and negative aspects of using contact lenses—the endless eye tests, maintenance, cleaning, storing and keeping up with the latest technology. But at the same time, it was great to be free of my heavy, thick glasses.

After cataract surgery in 2014, I seem to be free of any more eye issues. Out of all the things I have accomplished in my life—from graduating law school to years of piano lessons and playing at amateur events to serving as president of my condominium—one thing stands out ahead of everything else. That is simply because it has taken so many years for me to reach this point, when my eyes are no longer an issue.

Mission accomplished—finally!

# Heat!

I hate the hot weather! That may be because my grandparents were born in Eastern European countries where it is generally on the cold side. In addition to the heat, I hate summer clothes, the hot sun, sand, beaches and anything connected with the summer.

I have suffered two heat strokes in my life. The first one occurred on an island in the Galapagos where the air temperature consistently hovered in the 90's and 100's as our cruise ship group observed the local birds. All of a sudden, I began throwing up. The guide motioned for me to head for a bush rather than litter the pebbled pathway. Luckily, the ship's doctor was notified and I was brought in a motorboat back onboard, where he assisted me up the gangplank and to my room. He said that a combination of intense heat and dehydration probably caused my body to overheat. I was advised to rest and nibble on the fruit that had already been delivered to my room. Four hours later, I felt much better and was able to join the group for dinner.

I should have imprinted that experience in my mind for future trips, especially the one I took on a train through a national park in Utah. While walking through Park City in 100-degree heat, I was suddenly stricken and threw up. As soon as I returned to our train, which was air-conditioned (thankfully), I rested and drank as much water as I could. By the next morning, I felt fine.

Ever since then, I have carried water with me wherever I go, and even at home in New York City, I make a point of staying hydrated throughout the summer months. I stay in air-conditioned environments as much as I can.

I know there are people who cannot get enough of the hot sun and hate to see the summer end, but I am always happy for the opportunity to wear my fall and winter clothes, which means long walks through the city, even in the snow!

A day at the beach? No, thank you!

## Like Father, Unlike Daughter

When my father had a fatal heart attack in 1951, not too much was known in the medical field about these issues. When he originally learned that he had a heart condition, my father was simply advised to take it very easy. Considering his Type-A personality and penchant for perfection, this presented quite a challenge. As his condition worsened, his doctor told him to stop walking as much as possible. He redesigned our basement so that he could live in it and I have a vague recollection—I was about 14 years old—that he lived there only a short time before his fatal attack. According to my mother, remodeling was still going on and my father, who was displeased with the progress, was yelling at a worker just before he died.

This all occurred in an era before serious medical research into heart issues began, which changed after Dwight D. Eisenhower's heart attack in the late 50's. Now, of course, the landscape is entirely different and a significantly better body of knowledge exists to help people stay heart-healthy with exercise and healthy foods.

This is the opposite of the advice my father received, but it's become my model for healthy living. This process began in my thirties when, during a series of annual checkups, I was told that my blood pressure was elevated and that, at some point, I would have to start taking appropriate medication. Up until that time, I hadn't thought much about any genetic predisposition I may have had, that is, until I found out that my family history was probably the reason for my elevated blood pressure and that I should take precautions to keep my weight in check through diet and exercise. I was a couple of pounds overweight back then, due to a few too many expense account lunches.

So I began a quest to learn about healthy foods, especially those that are low in cholesterol, and I maintained an exercise program. However, in my 40's, I had to begin taking medication to keep my cholesterol levels and blood pressure at normal numbers. That worked for nearly 40 years as I passed yearly stress tests with flying colors and kept my blood pressure and cholesterol under control with medication.

Things changed in 2009. My annual stress test yielded some strange and frightening news, indicating that I had suffered a heart attack sometime since my most recent stress test. I never had any symptoms so I refused to accept this test result. My cardiologist urged me to take a heart scan where the technicians insert a dye, which allows them to see any plaque in the heart arteries that could cause an attack.

The scan report showed two main arteries filled with a large amount of plaque, which inhibits proper blood flow. My doctor ordered an angiogram, as it provides a better picture of the presence of plaque in the arteries surrounding the heart.

When he recommended this, I began having periodic backaches, chest pain and arm discomfort. Were these symptoms real? No one could say with any certainty.

Meanwhile, a planned trip to the Middle East was getting closer and my cardiologist was uncertain if I should go. I had travel insurance so I could cancel, but decided at the last minute to go. The trip ended up allowing me to forget about this health issue and with no symptoms at all the trip was a great experience.

Several weeks later, in January 2010, I had an angiogram. After a series of pre-op procedures—and signing my life away—I was wheeled into the procedure room. Someone numbed my arm so I would not feel a tube injected into a vein in my wrist, which was then pushed up my arm into my heart. The tube carried a small camera along with a shot of dye. I remained awake during this procedure and I was in no discomfort.

All of a sudden, the doctor performing the procedure left the room to have a conversation with my cardiologist and told me he would be right back. Ten minutes later—a very anxious ten minutes I might add—he returned with good news. Two main arteries contained plaque, but only 30 percent instead of 80 percent, meaning nothing needed to be done at the time.

He did say that I had a "branch line" with a large amount of plaque and he wanted to consult with my primary cardiologist about putting in a stent, which is a balloon that is inserted flat and then blown up when it's in the proper place. Then it keeps the wall linings separated so that plaque cannot fill the artery and cause a stroke or heart attack.

My cardiologist agreed that it should be done and the doctor performing the angiogram asked for my permission. He confirmed that I would not feel anything. I said I would agree if this would help my cardiologist take care of me. I wanted him to know as much as possible about the condition of my heart and its surrounding arteries.

The procedure involved retracting the tube that had already been inserted by way of a small puncture in a vein on my right wrist and reinserting the tube that contained the stent. While I felt no discomfort, I could feel something moving up my arm and through my chest. Most doctors prefer doing this procedure with an insertion in the groin area, which is easier to do but harder to recover from, but my doctor knew how to do the procedure through the arm which leaves virtually no after effects.

It was over quickly and I was wheeled back to pre-op where I waited for a bed. Apparently, New York State has a regulation that if you receive a stent you must remain in the hospital overnight. Throughout all of this, my niece,

Carol Sue, stayed with me. She even treated us to dinner from a local Italian restaurant before leaving the hospital and returning the next morning.

When I was discharged the next day, I felt great because at least for the moment the trauma was behind me. I now have a medical card that I must always carry. I don't know if the symptoms I had before this procedure were real or not, but I do know that I have had no symptoms since the day I received the stent.

I am currently doing cardio therapy, which requires three ten-minute sessions, three times a week. I work out on a treadmill, a rowing machine and an elliptical machine. These sessions are in addition to the exercise program I have been doing for years—water aerobics, balance and strength training, walking, meditation and yoga.

When I complete the cardio therapy, I plan to incorporate the routine into my time at the gym. Just before I left the hospital, I agreed to be part of a research effort on reducing stress. I spoke once a week with the founder of the research and learned how to deal with little or big situations of daily stress.

Now, at age 78, I believe I am in the best shape ever!

*Stitches!*

I once traveled with two friends to attend the annual Secretary of State Convention in Hershey, Pennsylvania. One of my friends knew these officials through business and invited us to join her for what she said would be a most enjoyable weekend.

When we arrived at the hotel in early afternoon, I announced that I wanted to go horseback riding. We arranged to meet for dinner in the hotel bar.

While I would not consider myself an equestrienne, I did take up riding back in the 1970's at Claremont Academy, which was once New York City's infamous riding school, located close to Central Park on the Upper West Side. I used to ride one night a week, which was not easy for me as I was afraid of the horses but always had a desire to learn how to ride.

As soon as I saw an opportunity to ride again at the hotel in Hershey, I decided to take advantage. I told the stable owner to consider me a beginner. I mounted the horse he had chosen and off we went on a trail clearly known to the horse. When we were out of sight of the stables the horse started to gallop along the trail. I became uncomfortable right away, but managed to hang on for the few minutes it took to return to the stables.

"My goodness you are back early," the owner said. "Since you have a half hour left, why not repeat the trail?"

I wasn't sure I wanted to do that after the ride I just had but I veered the horse toward the trail anyway and quickly realized that he did not want to go on that trail and instead headed toward the corral. But the gate was closed and when the horse realized that he turned his head in a very jerky motion to avoid hitting the gate. That movement threw me off his back.

Luckily, the horse stopped in its tracks and did not try to step on me as I lay on the ground. The owner rushed over and told me not to move, to just lay quiet. I was doing that when apparently he saw blood coming from the back of my head.

"We have to get you to a doctor," he said.

"Absolutely not," I said, having no idea that he saw blood.

I asked him to take me back to the hotel because I was feeling a little wobbly but otherwise fine. He reluctantly agreed.

Back inside the hotel, which was a short drive away, I was walking toward the elevators until a concierge stopped me because he saw that I was trailing blood on the lobby floor. He insisted that I be taken to Hershey Hospital. I was worried about meeting my friends at the bar but when I saw the blood I agreed to go.

At the hospital I was put on a gurney and left to wait in a hallway. Then someone wheeled me into a room, asked me what happened and set me up for an X-ray. After that was taken, I waited for a doctor to stitch me up. By then, the bleeding had stopped and I wasn't in any pain.

I waited and waited, and then I waited some more until I decided I had waited long enough. I stood up and walked into the hall and saw a room where two technicians were studying some X-rays.

"Oh my!" one of them said.

Then they turned toward me and from their facial expression I concluded that the "oh my" had something to do with me. I fainted and fell to the floor.

Next thing I knew, a doctor was waking me up, telling me I would be spending the night in the hospital so they could monitor me. Meanwhile, a neurologist was reviewing the x-rays of my head because the technicians had seen an enlarged brain scan and did not know exactly what it meant.

Not long after this frightening news, I was wheeled into a room and introduced to a doctor who told me that since there are no nerves in the brain my stitches could be done without anesthesia and that all I would feel is a few pricks here and there.

That worried me but I got through that procedure. They insisted that I stay overnight and I replied that I wanted to do no such thing. It was already 7 p.m. While that argument was taking place, I heard my two friends calling my name as they came down the hall.

"How did you know I was here?"

"When you didn't show up at the bar, we waited awhile and then asked the concierge if anyone had seen you. He hadn't, but he did describe an incident in which a young boy had fallen off a horse and was taken to the local hospital."

"Really?" I said.

My friends knew that was me because in those days I could pass for a boy, especially with my very short hair and no makeup. We all had a good laugh. Then we waited to hear what the neurologist had to say. He told us there was nothing wrong with me but that I did have an enlarged-sized brain. Apparently, that did not mean there was any serious problem. I could leave the hospital if I promised to come back in a couple of days so that the staff could check the stitches and see how I was faring.

I told my friends that I intended to get back on a horse as soon as possible, just to prove that this event hadn't scared me off riding. They totally disapproved but before our weekend was over I went anyway on a very easy and slow trail.

Luckily, over the next several years, all my other riding events were fun and accident-free, including a donkey ride on Mykonos Island in Greece, an infamous elephant ride in India and a mountain trail on horseback in Alaska that was simply beautiful.

But that's another story...

*Reflections*

## Morning Routine

FOR MANY YEARS, while working full-time at a corporation or law firm, my morning routine began with a 7:30 a.m. alarm clock, followed by a quick shower, getting dressed, grabbing breakfast and racing out the door. If I were ready with any time to spare, I would skim the paper.

Once I began doing work in my home office, my routine changed dramatically.
Instead of forcing myself to get out of bed at 7:30 sharp each day, I now wake up without an alarm at 5:30 a.m., feeling fully rested. This way, I get to spend the morning doing the things I like best.

My cats awake with me, even though they do not sleep in my bed. We all head to the kitchen, where I prepare coffee while they patiently wait for their morning food. I then open my front door and retrieve the newspaper. I set their food down and refresh their water bowl while my coffee is brewing. I also clean the litter box.

The coffee is usually ready by that point. I bring my mug and paper to the couch, turn on the TV for the morning news and start to read the paper. At some point, I'll decide what to have for breakfast, prepare it and return to the couch to eat as I read. This routine lasts until around 9:30 or 10, depending on how much of the paper I want to read.

What I love now about this time of day is that I no longer have to get up with that "I need to rush" feeling. I dealt with that for more than 40 years and now I am definitely grateful that I can wake up without that pressure. In fact, I still reflect each day about how nice it is to have this revised, easy-going morning routine.

## A Love Affair with Autumn

Whenever autumn arrives, it comes with a feeling that the year is just beginning. That may be the case for me because I was born in October!

I love the fall weather.

On the other hand, I hate the summer months. The heat slows me down physically and mentally. Even a workout at the gym is a strain. I don't like summer clothes, either. And I cannot sit in the sun because my skin is so fair. In fact, I could skip summer altogether.

Winter can be delightful. I love winter clothes, and as long as I have a warm coat, which I do, I am very comfortable in the cold weather. Perhaps this is due to my eastern European background. My favorite holiday comes on the heels of winter. Thanksgiving Day is a non-religious but patriotic holiday and it's when I eat exactly what I want. This includes kielbasa, an otherwise greasy and forbidden food.

Spring can be very pleasant *if* we even have one. Some years, it seems that we go directly from winter to summer all too quickly with maybe only a day or two of any weather resembling spring.

So like I said before, once the heat of summer has generally dissipated, the cooler weather of autumn has a way of invigorating me so I can move and react a lot faster. Even my favorite colors are associated with fall, particularly orange. Years ago, I took a popular course to learn about the colors that suit a person best, like for your skin and clothes and inner spirit. Mine were all connected to fall. I had been concerned that I would be told that pink and blue and black were my true colors, so I was quite happy to find that the colors I have in my home—yellows, oranges, off-white and beige—are my authentic colors.

Another thing I love about autumn is that cultural institutions in New York City, like the opera, ballet and orchestra, often start their new seasons in the fall.

No one can deny that the changing colors of the fall foliage require a scenic drive north of the city. I once spent a Sunday sailing north of Bear Mountain to view the leaves. It was definitely worth the trip, and I look forward to some version of it—by land or on water—each and every year.

The autumn even means a brand new season of television shows. Who can argue with a new fall lineup?

All of these are reasons why I love the fall and why New Year's means very little to me beyond remembering to change the year when I write a check and thinking about starting the paperwork for my tax returns.

Give me an October day forever!

# My To Do List

Some people believe that a formula for living is not to sweat the small stuff and that everything *is* small stuff. I could agree, except for one issue: end of life.

Since my family history has rendered me vulnerable to medical problems, like stroke and heart attacks, I am often concerned that I have not done enough to ensure that everything having to do with an illness or my death has been taken care of. Whether it is the money required to care for me and/or any funeral arrangements or personal wishes regarding my estate or medical directives, I need to have the money available and my wishes made known.

I guess I haven't done this yet because it's a big project. But I simply must. As a lawyer, I knew long ago that I should write my will to ensure this was all in place. It's now time to review the will to ensure that there is nothing I need to change. Although I won't change the distribution of my estate, which is to be distributed in three equal parts to my one nephew and two nieces, I do need to include an addendum that my niece, Alice Ann, gets first dibs on my furniture since we have similar tastes and she would probably appreciate having some of my pieces when the time comes.

I also have a healthcare proxy giving the power of attorney to Carol Sue. But I need to do an advance directive. Luckily, I did some volunteer work years ago as an ombudsman in a nursing home. Before undertaking the position, I had to take courses dealing with elder law and that is where I learned about advanced directives and the vocabulary one has to use so that doctors will understand exactly what is being dictated.

For example, I know I want to have a DNR (Do Not

Resuscitate) but this is not enough for a doctor. Suppose I have a stroke and wind up in what is called a "persistent vegetative state." Is this the time to begin the effectiveness of the DNR? I need to think about whether a "locked-in syndrome" where I cannot move or speak is appropriate to start the DNR. If it is clear that I am in a DNR state do I want to be moved out of a hospital setting to a member of the family for final care? While I do not want to put any burden on anyone, I will have to consider the pros and cons of this.

If I suffer from a heart attack, do I want to be given CPR and be subjected to all the lifesaving measures a hospital might administer? Or, do I say no to life support, endotracheal intubation, long-term mechanical ventilation, invasive procedures, intravenous fluids, feeding tubes and about 10 more items to consider and direct?

Finally, while I have considered donating my organs or entire body to science, I think I will most likely request cremation. Nevertheless, it's time to review all my documents to ensure that they represent exactly what I want.

Once I have completed this end of life project, I will turn my attention to completing my desire to visit 100 countries before any health issue prevents me from traveling, perhaps my biggest love in life.

I am grateful for all the opportunity I have had to see the world. The best part of my career was the traveling it allowed me to do. And if I wasn't traveling for work, I took vacation trips.

For me, traveling among different cultures has made me realize that there is no one way of thinking and that all people are struggling with the same issues of what, why and how to live one's life, which often means they turn to their respective religion to guide them along the way.

While I was raised Catholic, the church did not have the answers for me. Just before turning 30, I began a quest for my own answers, which has taken many years and included the study of many religions. Since I was never able to identify with any of them, I decided that living in the here and now was the best way for me.

This also means that I do not regret not marrying and not having children. My family has always been precious to me and I am forever grateful for them.

So there will be no need to shed any tears on the occasion of my passing because I have led a happy life. I am so thankful to be in a position that I can feel this way.

*On Spirituality*

On a trip to Japan I purchased an English version of what was known as "The Buddhist Bible," a short book that laid out the foundations of what it meant to be a Buddhist.

The Jesus Christ of Buddhism is Siddhartha Gautama. His mother died when he was born and this affected him deeply. Nevertheless, since his father was a king, he was brought up in luxury, got married at age 19 and continued living in the palace. When he left his home at age 29, he quickly grew upset by all the poverty he witnessed, and he subsequently decided to permanently leave the home he knew, his marriage and his only child. For years, he lived in various forests meditating and anticipating "enlightenment" (whatever that means). He is said to have reached this state of being after many years sitting under a tree in India.

I attended a Buddhist service in New York City but decided it was not for me.

At age 29, I had also left my home of sorts, since

I chose at that time to no longer observe the Catholic religion because I did not believe in its two basic tenets. First, that to achieve "salvation" (whatever that was) one had to be Roman Catholic. No other religion would do! The other was the issue of whether Mary was a virgin when her son, Jesus, was born. The Catholic Church refers to her as "The Virgin Mary."

The core of my problem was the issue of faith. One has to have faith in what one is being told in any particular religion because there is no proof. This was a prime example of why I realized that religious "business" was not for me.

I began a personal quest for spiritual fulfillment and to find a meaning in life that doesn't require a specific faith in something. My early travels abroad to European and Asian countries allowed me to conclude that I was not alone in my quest. I realized that people who were committed to some religion or body of thought felt that they had achieved their spiritual goals so there was nothing left for them to search for. People like me needed to find that religion or body of thought to obtain that sense of fulfillment.

I studied Theosophy (originated by a Russian woman named Blavatsky) with a "church" in New York City.

I followed Gurumay, a young lady with a huge following with ashrams in New York and India. She is supposedly "enlightened" but I was turned off from the kind of attention showered on her by her followers. It seemed to me like worshiping a celebrity instead of respecting an "all-knowing" person. I decided not to be a fan.

I went to groups like the Unitarians where you

can join and believe in whatever you want.

I visited Unity, where the premise is that Christ is in all of us rather than being apart from us.

I took courses at the School of Practical Philosophy on East 79th Street in New York City for a couple of years.

I studied French and found the pure sound of it to be a spiritual experience.

I read the books of Deepak Chopra, Thich Nhat Hannh (a Vietnamese Buddhist monk), Eckhart Tolle and other authors who strive for enlightenment through meditations that eliminate the ego.

I even obtained a mantra many years ago when I joined the Transcendental Meditation program that came to New York from India. I practiced meditation for years and occasionally still do.

My spiritual travels have taught me that while there is no one place for me each course of study has merit. Most important, after many years of searching, I am able to conclude that it does not matter that I haven't found a specific religion to follow or that I need to find a personal purpose for my existence.

Life is a work in progress. I am comfortable about how it is flowing for me. But I have never discarded the various bibles I have collected, including the Quran, because for some reason I feel that throwing out a religious book would be sacrilegious.

But that's another story...

*Gratitude*

## Love and Fear and Karma

I AM NOW 78 years old. In my quiet moments, I reflect on what has transpired in my life and what conclusions I can draw from my experiences.

After a lifetime encountering various religions, I have concluded that religion is a business like any other. I am an agnostic. I feel that there is a prime mover or initial catalyst in the universe, but after that we are on our own, and for me, that's fine. While there might be a purpose to our lives, it's probably still unintelligible to our current level of collective comprehension. Since I have stopped searching, I am finally comfortable *not* knowing if there is an afterlife.

As for love, what a complicated word! What does it mean? Feeling great chemistry with someone does not mean love because the chemistry is based on intangibles that stem from factors having nothing to do with love. For instance, one could be attracted to someone because he or she looks like one's parent or because someone is a strong individual, like one's mother or father.

I think that loving someone starts with attraction and timing and then one makes a commitment to make a relationship work. I think that love follows when each person makes the other feel respected in the context of committing to making the relationship work. Without that feeling, I don't see where the love is, and in my experience dealing with men who either lied or sought control, it certainly could not ultimately be found.

I feel very happy now that I did not live my life with fears about anything or anyone. At the same time, while I took on many challenges, I did not deliberately take that many big chances.

I started skiing when I was 40 years, but I did not accept the challenge of becoming an expert skier. I took up squash in my 30's, but did not accept the challenge of becoming a good player. I tried learning languages—German, French, Italian, Spanish and Russian—but never pursued them beyond what is known as "restaurant basics."

I completed more than half of the credits needed for a master's degree in law, but I never finished it. (Same for a master's in liberal arts.)

Of all the challenges I did pursue, swimming lessons after a childhood accident in which I nearly drowned is near the top of the list.

Traveling to foreign countries by myself has been a challenge, but I did it—over and over. It was a scary challenge to move to the U.K. and find a flat, a roommate and a job, but I did it.

Perhaps the hardest challenge I ever undertook was going to law school and passing the bar exam, which paved the way for a rewarding career.

I believe in karma. What you put out you get back. I think life should be lived by a moral and ethical code, and

I am comfortable knowing where I stand in that regard. In fact, I am looking for my next challenge right now.

## Wanted: A Crystal Ball!

I need a crystal ball to show me how the rest of my life will proceed, health-wise, so I can make decisions about how and where to live as I grow older. Up until now I didn't need or even want one as I was pretty much in control of my life, but as I age further I am concerned about possible heart issues (father) and dementia (mother), so I am thinking about how to continue living an independent and fulfilling life—with emphasis on independence.

If I knew what the future holds in terms of my health, I could be so much further along in planning how to spend the rest of my time here on earth. If I knew that I would succumb to a stroke or heart attack in a year, I would sell my apartment now and move closer to my family near Philadelphia. I am already on a waiting list at an adult (50+) community.

On the other hand, New York City is my favorite place in the world. I am an avid fan of the theater and nothing beats going to a first-class Broadway or off-Broadway play. The excitement of a live orchestra and live actors, stage sets and choreography all put together is wonderful. I have had subscriptions to the Metropolitan Opera House since 1963. I have been to the opera in Philadelphia and the difference in quality and staging is almost mind-boggling. There are fewer chorus singers, no elaborate stage settings, no particularly expensive costuming and fewer musicians in the orchestra, to name just a few.

*How could I ever leave New York?*

Since I ask this all the time, I do nothing about leaving and continue going to the theater, opera, ballet and museums. When I can, I ride the Staten Island ferry, which provides a marvelous view of the harbor and I go to Coney Island for a ride down memory lane. I did the parachute ride when I was about 15 with an uncle and was scared during the entire ride up as well as hitting the top and flying down. I liked it, but decided then and there that I would not go on that ride again and I never did. But I loved the cyclone roller coaster and enjoyed it many times over many years.

Meanwhile, my next learning curve may be finally mastering French. I have always wanted to speak that language and I hear that learning a new language is terrific mental exercise.

But I would really love to have a crystal ball.

## I Am Grateful For . . .

Passing the bar the first time.
Graduating from Columbia.
Graduating from Brooklyn Law.
Getting a film certificate.
Assisting JP with editing his summer film.
Living in London in the 60's.
Spending Christmas with the family.
Always having enough money.
That typing course after grade school.
My mother's advice about becoming a lawyer.
Doing the rough edit of *See Jane Run*
and then seeing it on TV.
Working on *Without Apology* and seeing screen credits.
My own practice.
Penny, my cat, for 12 years.
Leena and Neena for six years.
Gizmo and Harley who are still with me.
Being attractive.
Laser surgery on my eyes.
Good skin.
Paul, while it lasted.
Al, in the good times.
Independence.
Loretta, Pete and the kids.
Friendships of Gwen, Joy, Margie, Marilyn, Andrea.
Good health.
All the travels.

*Je ne regrette rien...*

*Moved to Tears*

Despite the fact that I love Bollywood movies and books written by Indian writers, I avoided visiting India for most of my traveling years because I felt it would be unnerving to witness the poverty and begging that India is known to have. But I bit that bullet in 2007 when I visited the northern part of the country, and again in 2008 when I traveled through the southern area.

Since I would be arriving in New Delhi around midnight local time, I assumed that the airport would be relatively empty. I was wrong! I walked out of the customs and baggage area into a sea of what appeared to be thousands of Indians apparently waiting for passengers to arrive. I kept looking for a placard with my name (I had prepaid for a car and driver to take me to the hotel) but found no one at first until I walked through a maze of Indians and finally saw my name.

What a relief! I had no local currency and was a

little apprehensive about what to do on my own. But all that subsided when I saw my driver.

I will never forget that crowd. Even Grand Central or Penn Station at their peak time cannot compare to the intense crowds at the New Delhi airport.

The second thing I did not expect was the absolutely stunning hotel and its grounds. It looked like what you would see on a perfect postcard of India. A concierge dressed in elaborate, colorful British clothing from the era when they ruled the country was surely a polar opposite to the shirts and jeans I had seen everyone wearing at the airport.

Even though it was two in the morning by this point, three young ladies in beautiful saris escorted me through the lobby to the reception area. They told me I could call on them for anything I might want or need. Looking around, I was moved to tears. This happens whenever I am suddenly overwhelmed by something of beauty or when I am thrilled to be at a place like Tiananmen Square in Beijing or Red Square in Moscow.

In fact I was moved to tears many times on my trips to India.

But that's another story...

## EPILOGUE

When I began traveling at the age of 20, I began collecting matchbooks from various places I had been, which I felt would conjure up the memory of those particular trips. In those days, smoking was popular and matchbooks could be found everywhere. I even planned to write a memoir using matchbooks as a trigger for memories of life and travel.

Each time I returned home from another trip I brought a collection of matchbooks and threw them in a large glass bowl. As it got full, I thought I might have to get rid of the matches and just keep the covers. But I was too busy in those days to get around to doing that little chore.

One year, I hired a young gentleman named Bob who had been recommended by a friend as a great domestic. I had never employed anyone as a domestic before but I decided it was a good idea. And despite the fact that he said, "Real men don't do laundry"—which meant he wouldn't do any of mine—I still took him on. He was anal and fastidious and for many years my apartment smelled clean and fresh with no hint of dust anywhere. He swept around and under all kinds of furniture. Whenever I returned home after a day at the office I knew Bob had been there.

All this time, my collection of matchbooks was getting closer and closer to the top of the glass bowl.

Years later, I came home one day after Bob had done the cleaning and I noticed that the bowl was empty. Not a matchbook to be found. I called him and asked if he had taken them and he said he had thrown them in the garbage.

"Why did you do that?"

He replied that they were a fire hazard and that he simply had to get rid of them.

"Didn't you notice that the matchbooks came from all over the world?"

I explained that this was my way of building a memoir of my trips. He refused to apologize and was unwavering in his insistence that this fire trap had to be dealt with even though he had been seeing them for years and had never asked about them or if he could destroy them.

A month later, I let him go. I was so angry that the thought of him continuing to come to my apartment caused my stress level to reach a place I was not able to handle. All those memories had just disappeared from view!

I continued to memorialize my trips with an 8 millimeter video camera with no sound, and then with a video camera (with sound) for my trip to China in 1972. After studying film, I purchased a professional video camera, which I used for my trips to Antarctica and India. I also kept a log of daily events on my trip to Dubai.

But I never forgot losing those matchbooks.

Several years ago, I attended a Sunday morning lecture at the Society for Ethical Culture and learned about a course on personal writing they were offering that I had always wanted to explore.

But that's another story...

## ACKNOWLEDGMENTS

I am so grateful to Elaine Berman Gurney, my writing teacher at the Ethical Culture Society, who encouraged us with a great deal of care and support. Without her, I would not have written these personal stories.

My first experience with an editor has been terrific. David Tabatsky enthusiastically took on this project and shared his vast range of experience in guiding me. I am most thankful to him.

I want to acknowledge the support of family members John Peter, Carol Sue and Alice Ann, who encouraged this project. I also thank two of my friends, Joy and Marilyn, who have supported me, too.

Finally, while I cannot thank the nuns at my grammar school for any kindness they showed me, or the company personnel who said it was their policy not to hire women lawyers or the men whose relationships caused me much emotional pain, I have to admit that each and every one of them have provided so much material to write about.